Anonymous

President's Message and accompanying Documents

To the Senate and House of Representatives of the Confederate States

Anonymous

President's Message and accompanying Documents
To the Senate and House of Representatives of the Confederate States

ISBN/EAN: 9783337173241

Printed in Europe, USA, Canada, Australia, Japan

Cover: Foto ©ninafisch / pixelio.de

More available books at **www.hansebooks.com**

PRESIDENT'S MESSAGE

AND

ACCOMPANYING DOCUMENTS.

To the Senate and House of Representatives of the Confederate States:

It is again our fortune to meet for devising measures necessary to the public welfare whilst our country is involved in a desolating war. The sufferings endured by some portions of the people excite the deep solicitude of the Government, and the sympathy thus evoked has been heightened by the patriotic devotion with which these sufferings have been borne. The gallantry and good conduct of our troops, always claiming the gratitude of the country, have been further illustrated on hard fought fields, marked by exhibitions of individual prowess which can find but few parallels in ancient or modern history. Our army has not faltered in any of the various trials to which it has been subjected, and the great body of the people have continued to manifest a zeal and unanimity which not only cheer the battle-stained soldier, but gives assurance to the friends of constitutional liberty of our final triumph in the pending struggle against despotic usurpation.

The vast army which threatened the capital of the Confederacy has been defeated and driven from the lines of investment, and the enemy repeatedly foiled in his efforts for its capture, is now seeking to raise new armies on a scale such as modern history does not record, to effect that subjugation of the South so often proclaimed as on the eve of accomplishment.

The perfidy which disregarded rights secured by compact, the madness which trampled on obligations made sacred by every consideration of honor, have been intensified by the malignity engendered by defeat. These passions have changed the character of the hostilities waged by our enemies, who are becoming daily less regardful of the usages of civilized war and the dictates of humanity. Rapine and wanton destruction of private property, war upon non-combatants, murder of captives, bloody threats to avenge the death of an invading soldiery by the slaughter of unarmed citizens, orders of banishment against peaceful farmers engaged in the cultivation of the soil, are some of the means used by our ruthless invaders to enforce the submission of a free people to foreign sway. Confiscation bills of a character so atrocious as to ensure, if executed, the utter ruin of the entire population of these States, are passed by their Congress and approved by their Executive. The moneyed obligations of the Confederate Government are forged by citizens of the United States, and publicly advertised for sale in their cities with a notoriety that sufficiently attests the knowledge of their Government, and its complicity in the crime is further evinced by the fact that the soldiers of the invading armies are found supplied with large quantities of these forged notes as a means of despoiling the country people, by fraud, out of such portions of their property as armed violence may fail to reach. Two at least of the generals of the United States are engaged, unchecked by their Government, in exciting servile insurrection, and in arming and training slaves for warfare against their masters, citizens of the Confederacy. Another has been found of instincts so brutal as to invite the violence of his soldiery against the women of a captured city. Yet the rebuke of civilized man has failed to evoke from the authorities of the United States one mark of disapprobation of his acts, nor is there any reason to suppose that the conduct of Benjamin F. Butler has failed to secure from his Government the sanction and applause with which it is known to have been greeted by public meetings and portions of the press of the United States. To inquiries made of the commander-in-chief of the armies of the United States whether the atrocious conduct of some of their military commanders met the sanction of that Government, answer has been evaded on the pretext that the enquiry was insulting, and no method remains for the repression of these enormities but such retributive justice as it may be found possible to execute. Retaliation in kind for many of them is impracticable, for I have had occasion to remark in a former message that under no excess of provocation could our noble hearted defenders be driven to wreak vengeance on unarmed men, on women, or on children. But stern and exemplary punishment can and must be meted out to the murderers and felons who, disgracing the profession of arms, seek to make of public war the occasion for the commission of the most monstrous crimes. Deeply as we may regret the character of the contest into which we are about to be forced, we must accept it as an alternative which recent manifestations give us little reason to hope can be avoided. The exasperation of failure has aroused the worst passions of our enemies: a large portion of their people, even of the clergymen, now engage in urging an excited populace to the extreme of ferocity, and nothing remains but to vindicate our rights and maintain our existence by employing against our foes every energy and every resource at our disposal.

I append for your information a copy of the papers exhibiting the action of the Government up to the present time for the repression of the outrages committed on our people. Other measures now in progress will be submitted hereafter.

In inviting your attention to the legislation which the necessities of our condition require, those connected with the prosecution of the war command almost undivided attention. The acts passed at your last session intended to secure the public defence by general enrolment, and to render uniform the rules governing troops in the service, have led to some unexpected criticism that is much to be regretted. The efficacy of the law has thus been somewhat impaired, though it is not believed that in any of the States the popular mind has withheld its sanction from either the necessity or propriety of your legislation. It is only by harmonious as well as zealous action that a government as now as ours, ushered into existence on the very eve of a great war, and unprovided with the material necessary for conducting hostilities on so vast a scale, can fulfil its duties. Upon you who are fully informed of the acts and purposes of the Government, and thoroughly imbued with the feelings and sentiments of the people, must reliance be placed to secure this great object. You can best devise the means for establishing that entire co-operation of the State and Confederate Governments which is essential to the well-being of both at all times, but which is now indispensable to their very existence. And if any legislation shall seem to you appropriate for adjusting differences of opinion, it will be my pleasure as well as duty, to co-operate in any measure that may be devised for reconciling a just care for the public defence with a proper deference for the most scrupulous susceptibilities of the State authorities.

The report of the Secretary of the Treasury will exhibit in detail the operations of that department. It will be seen with satisfaction that the credit of the Government securities remains unimpaired, and that this credit is fully justified by the comparatively small amount of accumulated debt, nothwithstanding the magnitude of our military operations. The legislation of the last session provided for the purchase of supplies with the bonds of the Government, but the preference of the people for Treasury Notes has been so marked that legislation is recommended to authorize an increase in the issue of Treasury Notes, which the public service seems to require. No grave inconvenience need be apprehended from this increased issue, as the provision of law by which these notes are convertible into eight per cent. bonds, forms an efficient and permanent safeguard against any serious depreciation of the currency. Your attention is also invited to the means proposed by the Secretary for facilitating the preparation of these notes, and for guarding them against forgery. It is due to our people to state that no manufacture of counterfeit notes exists within our limits, and that they are all imported from the Northern States.

The report of the Secretary of War, which is submitted, contains numerous suggestions for the legislation, deemed desirable in order to add to the efficiency of the service. I invite your favorable consideration especially to those recommendations, which are intended to secure the proper execution of the Conscript Law, and the consolidation of companies, battalions and regiments, when so reduced in strength as to impair that uniformity of organization which is necessary in the army, while an undue burthen is imposed on the Treasury. The necessity for some legislation for controlling military transportation on the railroads, and improving their present defective condition forces itself upon the attention of the Government, and I trust that you will be able to devise satisfactory measures for attaining this purpose.

The legislation on the subject of general officers involves the service in some difficulties which are pointed out by the Secretary, and for which the remedy suggested by him seems appropriate.

In connection with this subject, I am of opinion that prudence dictates some provision for the increase of the army, in the event of emergencies not now anticipated. The very large increase of forces recently called into the field by the President of the United States may render it necessary hereafter to extend the provisions of the Conscript Law so as to embrace persons between the ages of 35 and 45 years. The vigor and efficiency of our present forces, their condition, and the skill and ability which distinguish their leaders inspire the belief that no further enrolment will be necessary, but a wise foresight requires that if a necessity should be suddenly developed during the recess of Congress, requiring increased forces for our defence, means should exist for calling such forces into the field without awaiting the re-assembling of the Legislative Department of the Government.

In the election and appointment of officers for the Provisional Army, it was to be anticipated that mistakes would be made and incompetent officers of all grades introduced into the service. In the absence of experience, and with no reliable guide for selection, executive appointments as well as elections have been sometimes unfortunate. The good of the service, the interests of our country require, that some means be devised for withdrawing the commission of officers who are incompetent for the duties required by the position, and I trust that you will find means for relieving the army of such officers by some mode more prompt and less wounding to their sensibility than judgment of a court martial.

Within a recent period we have effected the object so long desired of an arrangement for the exchange of prisoners, which is now being executed by delivery at the points agreed upon, and which will, it is hoped, speedily restore our brave and unfortunate countrymen to their places in the ranks of the army, from which by the fortune of war they have for a time been separated. The details of this arrangement will be communicated to you in a special report when further progress has been made in their execution.

Of other particulars concerning the operations of the War Department, you will be informed by the Secretary in his report and the accompanying documents

The report of the Secretary of the Navy, embraces a statement of the operations and present condition of this branch of the public service, both afloat and ashore; the construction and equipment of armed vessels at home and abroad; the manufacture of ordnance and ordnance stores; the establishment of workshops and the development of our resources of coal and of iron. Some legislation seems essential for securing crews for vessels. The difficulties now experienced on this point are fully stated in the Secretary's report, and I invite your attention to providing a remedy.

The report of the Postmaster General discloses the embarrassments which resulted in the postal service from the occupation by the enemy of the Mississippi River and portions of the territory of the different States. The measures taken by the department for relieving these embarrassments as far as practicable, are detailed in the report. It is a subject of congratulation, that during the ten months which ended on the 31st March last, the expenses of the department were largely decreased, whilst its revenue was augmented, as compared with a corresponding period ending on the 30th June, 1860, when the postal service for these States was conducted under the authority delegated to the United States. Sufficient time has not yet elapsed to determine whether the measures, heretofore devised by Congress, will accomplish the end of bringing the expenditures of the department within the limit of its own revenues by the first of March next, as required by the Constitution.

I am happy to inform you, that in spite both of blandishments and threats, used in profusion by the agents of the government of the United States, the Indian nations within the Confederacy, have remained firm in their loyalty and steadfast in the observance of their treaty engagements with this government. Nor has their fidelity been shaken by the fact that, owing to the vacancies in some of the offices of Agents and Superintendents, delay has occurred in the payments of the annuities and allowances to which they are entitled. I I would advise some provision authorizing payments to be made by other officers, in the absence of those specially charged by law with this duty.

We have never-ceasing cause to be grateful for the favor with which God has protected our infant Confederacy. And it becomes us, reverently to return our thanks and humbly to ask of his bounteousness that wisdom which is needful for the performance of the high trusts with which we are charged.

JEFFERSON DAVIS.

Richmond, August 15th, 1862.

HEADQUARTERS ARMY OF THE C. S.,

NEAR RICHMOND, VA.,

August 2, 1862.

To the General Commanding U. S. Army, Washington :

GENERAL : In obedience to the order of his Excellency, the President of the Confederate States, I have the honor to make to you the following communication :

On the 22d of July last a cartel for a general exchange of prisoners of war was signed by Major General John A. Dix, on behalf of the United States, and by Major General D. H. Hill, on the part of this Government. By the terms of that cartel it is stipulated that all prisoners of war hereafter taken, shall be discharged on parole, until exchanged.

Scarcely had the cartel been signed when the military authorities of the United States commenced a practice changing the character of the war, from such as becomes civilized nations, into a campaign of indiscriminate robbery and murder.

A General Order issued by the Secretary of War of the United States in the City of Washington, on the very day that the cartel was signed in Virginia, directs the military commander of the United States to take the property of our people for the convenience and use of the army, without compensation.

A General Order issued by Major General Pope, on the 23d of July last, the day after the date of the cartel, directs the murder of our peaceful citizens as spies, if found quietly tilling their farms in his rear, *even outside of his lines.*

And one of his Brigadier Generals, Steinwehr, has seized innocent and peaceful inhabitants to be held as hostages, to the end that they may be murdered in cold blood, if any of his soldiers are killed by some unknown persons, whom he designated as "bushwhackers."

Some of the military authorities of the United States seem to suppose that their end will be better attained by a savage war, in which no quarter is to be given and no age or sex to be spared, than by such hostilities as are alone recognized to be lawful in modern times. We find ourselves driven by our enemies, by steady progress, towards a practice which we abhor, and which we are vainly struggling to avoid.

Under these circumstances this government has issued the accompanying General Order, which I am directed by the President to transmit to you, recognizing Major General Pope and his commissioned officers to be in the position which they have chosen for themselves, that of robbers and murderers, and not that of public enemies, entitled, if captured, to be treated as prisoners of war.

The President also instructs me to inform you that we renounce our right of retaliation on the innocent, and will continue to treat the private enlisted soldiers of General Pope's army as prisoners of war; but if, after notice to your government that we confine repressive measures to the punishment of commissioned officers, who are willing participants in these crimes, the savage practices threatened in the orders alluded to, be persisted in, we shall reluctantly be forced to the last resort of accepting the war on the terms chosen by our enemies, until the voice of an outraged humanity shall compel a respect for the recognized usages of war. While the President considers that the facts referred to would justify a refusal on our part to execute the cartel, by which we have agreed to liberate an excess of prisoners of war in our hands, a sacred regard for plighted faith, which shrinks from the semblance of breaking a promise, precludes a resort to such an extremity. Nor is it his desire to extend to any other forces of the United States the punishment merited by General Pope and such commissioned officers as choose to participate in the execution of his infamous orders.

I have the honor to be,

Very respectfully,

Your obedient servant,

(Signed)   R. E. LEE,

General Commanding.

ADJUTANT AND INSPECTOR GENERAL'S OFFICE,
Richmond, August 1, 1862.

GENERAL ORDERS, }
   No. 54.   }

I. The following Orders are published for the information and observance of all concerned:

II. Whereas, by a General Order, dated the 22d July 1862, issued by the Secretary of War of the United States, under the order of the President of the United States, the military commanders of that government within the states of Virginia, South Carolina, Georgia, Florida, Alabama, Mississippi, Louisiana, Texas and Arkansas, are directed to seize and use any property, real or personal, belonging to the inhabitants of this Confederacy, which may be necessary or convenient for their several commands, and no provision is made for any compensation to the owners of private property thus seized and appropriated by the military commanders of the enemy:

III. And whereas, by General Order number eleven, issued on the 23d July 1862, by Major General Pope, commanding the forces of the enemy in Northern Virginia, it is ordered that all "commanders of army corps, divisions, brigades and detached commands, will proceed immediately to arrest all disloyal male citizens within their lines or within their reach, in rear of their respective commands. Such as are willing to take the oath of allegiance to the United States, and will furnish sufficient security for its observance, shall be permitted to remain at their homes, and pursue in good faith their accustomed avocations. Those who refuse, shall be conducted South, beyond the extreme pickets of this army, and be notified that if found again any where within our lines, or at any point in rear, they will be considered spies, and subjected to the extreme rigor of military law. If any person having taken the oath of allegiance as above specified, be found to have violated it, he shall be shot, and his property seized and applied to the public use:"

IV. And whereas, by an order issued on the 13th July 1862, by Brigadier General A. Steinwehr, Major William Steadman, a cavalry officer of his brigade, has been ordered to arrest five of the most prominent citizens of Page county, Virginia, to be held as hostages, and to suffer death in the event of any of the soldiers of said Steinwehr being shot by "bushwhackers," by which term are meant the citizens of this Confederacy who have taken up arms to defend their homes and families:

V. And whereas it results from the above orders that some of the military authorities of the United States, not content with the unjust and aggressive warfare hitherto waged with savage cruelty against an unoffending people, and exasperated by the failure of their effort to subjugate them, have now determined to violate all the rules and usages of war, and to convert the hostilities hitherto waged against armed forces into a campaign of robbery and murder against unarmed citizens and peaceful tillers of the soil :

VI. And whereas this government, bound by the highest obligations of duty to its citizens, is thus driven to the necessity of adopting such just measures of retribution and retaliation as shall seem adequate to repress and punish these barbarities ; and whereas the orders above recited have only been published and made known to this government since the signature of a cartel for exchange of prisoners of war, which cartel, in so far as it provides for an exchange of prisoners hereafter captured, would never have been signed or agreed to by this government, if the intention to change the war into a system of indiscriminate murder and robbery had been made known to it: and whereas a just regard to humanity forbids that the repression of crime which this government is thus compelled to enforce should be unnecessarily extended to retaliation on the enlisted men in the army of the United States, who may be the unwilling instruments of the savage cruelty of their commanders, so long as there is hope that the excesses of the enemy may be checked or prevented by retribution on the commissioned officers who have the power to avoid guilty action, by refusing service under a government which seeks their aid in the perpetration of such infamous barbarities :

VII. Therefore, it is ordered that Major General Pope, Brigadier General Steinwehr, and all commissioned officers serving under their respective commands, be and they are hereby expressly and specially declared to be not entitled to be considered as soldiers, and therefore not entitled to the benefit of the cartel for the parole of future prisoners of war. Ordered further, that in the event of the capture of Major General Pope, or Brigadier General Steinwehr, or of any commissioned officer serving under them, the captive so taken shall be held in close confinement so long as the orders aforesaid shall continue in force and unrepealed by the competent military authorities of the United States : and that in the event of the murder of any unarmed citizen or inhabitant of this Confederacy by virtue or under pretext of any of the orders hereinbefore recited, whether with or without trial, whether under pretence of such citizen being a spy or hostage, or any other pretence, it shall be the duty of the Commanding General of the forces of this Confederacy to cause immediately to be hung, out of the commissioned officers, prisoners as aforesaid, a number equal to the number of our own citizens thus murdered by the enemy.

By order.

S. COOPER,
Adjutant and Inspector General.

CONFEDERATE STATES OF AMERICA,
WAR DEPARTMENT,
Richmond, June 29, 1862.

General R. E. LEE,
Commanding Department of Northern Virginia :

GENERAL : When you send a flag of truce again there are two matters which I wish to bring to the notice of the general in command of the U. S. forces, for the consideration of his government.

We have seen in the Northern papers that Mr. Wm. B. Mumford, of New Orleans, and Colonel Owens, of the Missouri State Guard, have been executed by the U. S. authorities, Mr. Mumford for having pulled down the U. S. flag in New Orleans, and Colonel Owens upon a charge of bridge burning in Missouri. The former was hung, the latter was shot.

We are informed that Mr. Mumford pulled the flag down when the enemy were not yet in possession of the city, but had merely anchored their vessels before it, and had made a demand for a surrender, which had not been complied with.

A party landed, hoisted the flag, and retired. The city was not in their possession, nor subject to their jurisdiction. Under such circumstances the execution of Mr. Mumford was the murder of one of our citizens. I enclose the account of his execution from the New Orleans Delta.

We are informed that Colonel Owens was shot without trial. Such is the account given in the Missouri papers, as you will perceive from the enclosed slip, containing an extract from the Hannibal Herald. He was a duly commissioned officer of the Second Division of the Missouri State Guard.

We have executed private individuals for burning bridges, and persons in military service for coming disguised within our lines to destroy railroads, but we have given them fair trials.

If Colonel Owens entered the enemy's lines in disguise and burned bridges, we could not consistently deny their right to try and punish him, but an execution without trial is not justifiable under any circumstances, and if he acted in obedience to orders and without entering the lines of the enemy in disguise, his execution is a palpable murder, committed by a U. S. officer.

Supposing Mr. Mumford, a citizen of the Confederate States, to have been executed for an insult to the U. S. flag, hoisted in a city not in their possession, and Colonel Owens to have been executed without trial, we deem it our duty to call on the authorities of the U. S. for a statement of the facts, inasmuch as we do not intend to permit outrages of that character to be perpetrated without retaliation.

Very respectfully,
Your obedient servant,
(Signed)   GEO. W. RANDOLPH,
Secretary of War.

HEADQUARTERS ARMY OF THE C. S.,

NEAR RICHMOND, VA.,

August 2, 1862.

To the General Commanding U. S. Army, Washington :

GENERAL.: On the 29th of June last, I was instructed by the Secretary of War to enquire of Major-General McClellan, as to the truth of alleged murders committed on our citizens by officers of the U. S. Army. The cases of Wm. B. Mumford, reported to have been murdered at New Orleans by order of Major-General B. F. Butler, and Colonel John Owens, reported to have been murdered in Missouri, by order of Major-General Pope, were those referred to. I had the honor to be informed by Major-General McClellan that he had referred these inquiries to his Government for a reply. No answer has as yet been received.

The President of the Confederate States has since been credibly informed that numerous other officers of the Army of the U. S. within the Confederacy, have been guilty of felonies and capital offences which are punishable by all laws human and divine. I am directed by him to bring to your notice a few of those best authenticated. Newspapers received from the United States announce as a fact, that Major-General Hunter has armed slaves for the murder of their masters, and has thus done all in his power to inaugurate a servile war, which is worse than that of the savage, inasmuch as it superadds other horrors to the indiscriminate slaughter of all ages, sexes and conditions.

Brigadier-General Phelps is reported to have initiated at New Orleans the example set by Major-General Hunter on the coast of South Carolina.

Brigadier-General G. N. Fitch is stated in the same journals to have murdered in cold blood two peaceful citizens because one of his men while invading our country, was killed by some unknown person defending his home.

I am instructed by the President of the Confederate States to repeat the enquiry relative to the cases of Mumford and Owens, and to ask whether the statements in relation to the action of Generals Hunter, Phelps and Fitch are admitted to be true; and whether the conduct of these Generals is sanctioned by their Government.

I am further directed by His Excellency the President, to give notice that in the event of not receiving a reply to these enquiries within fifteen days from the delivery of this letter, that it will be assumed that the alleged facts are true, and are sanctioned by the Government of the United States.

In such event, on that Government will rest the responsibility of the retribution or retaliatory measures which shall be adopted to put an end to the merciless atrocities which now characterize the war waged against the Confederate States.

I am, most respectfully,

Your obedient servant,

(Signed)   R. E. LEE,
                                                    General Commanding.

(Copy.)

HEADQUARTERS OF THE ARMY,

WASHINGTON, *August* 7, 1862.

General R. E. LEE,

    Commanding, &c. :

GENERAL: Your letter of July 6th was received at the Adjutant General's Office on the 14th, but supposing from its endorsement that it required no further reply, it was filed without being shown to the President or Secretary of War. I learned to-day for the first time that such letter had been received and hasten to reply.

No authentic information has been received in relation to the execution of either John Owens or ——— Mumford, but measures will be immediately taken to ascertain the facts of these alleged executions of which you will be duly informed.

I need hardly assure you, General, that so far as the United States authorities are concerned, this contest will be carried on in strict accordance with the laws and usages of modern warfare, and that all excesses will be duly punished.

In regard to the burning of bridges, &c., within our lines by persons in disguise as peaceful citizens, I refer you to my letter of January 22d last to General Price. I think you will find the views there expressed as not materially differing from those stated in your letter.

In regard to retaliation by taking the lives of innocent persons, I know of no modern authority which justifies it, except in the extreme case of a war with an uncivilized foe which has himself established first such a barbarous rule. The United States will never countenance such a proceeding, unless forced to do so by the barbarous conduct of an enemy who first applies such a rule to our own citizens.

    Very respectfully,

        Your obedient servant,

(Signed)   H. W. HALLECK,

                    General-in-Chief U. S. Army.

HEADQUARTERS OF THE ARMY,

WASHINGTON, *August 9th*, 1862.

General R. E. LEE,

 Commanding, &c. :

 GENERAL: Your two communications of the 2d inst., with enclosures are received. As these papers are couched in language exceedingly insulting to the Government of the United States, I must respectfully decline to receive them. They are herewith returned.

  Very respectfully,

   Your obedient servant,

(Signed)   H. W. HALLECK,

         General-in-Chief U. S. Army.

REPORT OF THE SECRETARY OF WAR.

CONFEDERATE STATES OF AMERICA,
War Department,
Richmond, August 12th, 1862.

To His Excellency JEFFERSON DAVIS,
President of the Confederate States.

SIR: Although it is not customary for the heads of departments to make reports at extra sessions of Congress, yet, in consideration of recent changes in the organization of the Army, and of the necessity for further legislation, it is deemed best to depart from this usage on the present occasion.

It became apparent, in the course of the last Spring, to all acquainted with the condition of the Army, that the acts of Congress, providing for re-enlistments, would not effect the desired object. The privilege allowed of re-enlisting for different corps, and even for different arms of the service, coupled with the love of change always found in camps, and heightened in the case of our armies by the monotony and discomfort of winter quarters, caused such extensive changes, that the re-enlistments tended to the disorganization of the Army.

Large numbers of our men, yearning for home, weary of the discomfort of camp life, and deceived by the apparent inactivity of the enemy into the belief that their services were no longer necesary, declined to re-enlist and prepared to turn over the burden of the war to those who had as yet borne no part of it. Efforts to procure re-enlistments and the expectation of change, relaxed the discipline of the Army, impaired its efficiency, and rendered it incapable of accomplishing what otherwise might have been achieved.

While our armies were thus passing through successive stages of disorganization to dissolution, those of the enemy recruited and re-organized, had reached a high state of efficiency, and were ready at the opening of the campaign to enter upon it, with every guarantee of success that numbers, discipline, complete organization and perfect equipments could afford.

The success they obtained under these circumstances, far from being a matter of surprise, were necessary consequences of the relative conditions of the armies, and it is truly surprising that these successes were not greater and more complete.

The plan of voluntary enlistment having failed to preserve the organization, and to recruit the strength of our armies at a time when the safety of the country required both to be effected, a resort to draft or conscription was the only alternative. To all acquainted with the true condition of things there could be no ground for doubt. In a period of thirty days the terms of service of one hundred and forty-eight regiments expired. There was good reason to believe that a large majority of the men had not re-enlisted, and of those who had re-enlisted, a very large majority had entered corps which could never be assembled, or if assembled, could not be prepared for the field in time to meet the invasion actually commenced.

There was, therefore, an interval of disorganization and weakness impending, and the enemy had already entered Virginia with an army, now known to have had more than double the numerical strength of our own and superior to it in everything but courage and a good cause. It was obvious that conscription alone could save us, and it could hardly be supposed that a Constitution adopted in the midst of war, inhibited the only possible mode of raising armies.

Influenced by these and other considerations, Congress adopted the measure popularly known as the Conscript Act. Four months have not elapsed since its passage and the present condition of the army and of the country sufficiently prove its wisdom. Four months ago our armies were retiring weak and disorganized before the overwhelming force of the enemy, yielding to them the sea-coast, the mines, the manufacturing power, the grain fields, and even entire States of the Confederacy. Now we are advancing with increased numbers, improving organization, renewed courage and the prestige of victory, upon an enemy defeated, disheartened, and sheltering himself behind defensive works and under cover of his gun-boats. A military system which has done so much in so short a time, should be cherished and perfected, and its defects speedily corrected.

Soon after the passage of the Conscript Act, the department prepared to carry it out, and on the 28th of April, published General Order No. 30, a copy of which is herewith returned, prescribing regulations for the enrolment, mustering in, subsistence, transportation and disposition of conscripts.

It was determined to establish one or more permanent camps in each State, at points selected with reference to health and facilities for subsistence and transportation. Each camp has its Commanding officer, its Drill officers, its Commissary, Quartermaster and Surgeon. The conscripts are to be assembled, drilled, taken through the camp diseases, and distributed among the regiments of the State in proportion to their respective deficiencies.

The necessity of sending them immediately into the field, has interfered with this plan of operations, but it has been carried out as far as practicable, and during any period of comparative inactivity it can be fully executed. Recruits thus prepared for the field, will be little inferior to old soldiers, and the army will be relieved from its crowded hospitals and the long train of ineffectives that now drags in its rear.

The greatest difficulty encountered in the execution of the law, has been that which constitutes the chief impediment in all involuntary military systems, the enrolment of recruits. The third section of the Act requires the enrolling officers of the State to be used with the consent of the respective Governors, and it is only on failure to obtain such consent, that the President is authorized to employ Confederate officers.

The military systems of many of the States are fallen into such disuse, that there are either no enrolling officers, or none that can be relied on. So far the experiment of using State officers has proved a failure, and I would suggest that permission be given to resort to other measures for enrolling recruits.

This may be done either by the appointment of a certain number of enrolling officers for each Congressional District, or by giving each corps supernumerary officers to act as enrolling officers for the corps. The latter plan would probably give more activity and efficiency to enrolments than the former, as the enrolling officers would be under military control, and if inefficient, might be ordered back to their regiments and be substituted by others.

The 4th and 13th sections of the act require all conscripts and volunteers to enter companies in existence at the passage of the act, thus cutting off recruits for companies mustered into service after that time. The object of this restriction was apparent, the new companies then forming were allowed thirty days to complete their organization, and had the advantage over companies in the field in recruiting. It was supposed necessary, therefore, to restore equality by giving the conscripts and volunteers after thirty days to the old companies.

The effect will be, that many fine regiments brought into service since the passage of the act will go down for the want of recruits. I think it will be well to permit conscripts to be assigned and volunteers to enter all companies in service.

It is true that the number of regiments is already too great, and that it is impossible to keep them all up. This may have been a motive for restricting recruits to old regiments and permitting the others gradually to decline. But it will be better to discriminate in the reduction of the number of regiments, and to consolidate such as become too weak to be recruited. The power of consolidating regiments, battalions, and companies, is so essential that our armies cannot be maintained in a tolerable state of efficiency without its exercise. The Department has been compelled to disband corps because useless from loss of men or other cause, but as the law now stands, this can only be done by discharging the entire corps and enrolling the men within the conscript age for service in other companies.

Two inconveniences attend this mode of proceeding: First, all the men over thirty-five and under eighteen are lost, even though they have enlisted for the war. Secondly, it is doubtful whether conscripts can be enrolled out of their own States, and a company, therefore, cannot be disbanded out of the State in which it was raised without losing the whole company.

I suggest, therefore, that whenever a corps becomes so much reduced as to be unfit for service, and there is no reasonable expectation of recruiting it, the President be authorized to disband it, to put the officers out of commission and to transfer the non-commissioned officers and privates to other corps from the same State. It may be objected that this violates the contract of enlistment which is for service in

2

the company selected by the volunteer, and thus the Government, in accepting the volunteer, impliedly engages to keep him in the company of his choice. I think that the engagement of the Government is fulfilled by retaining the volunteer in his company so long as it is fit for service, but that there is no implied promise to discharge him when his company can be no longer preserved. Such a promise would be a premium to inefficiency. A company anxious to leave the service would secure its object by rendering itself unfit to remain.

I also further recommend that power be given to enrol conscripts wherever they may bo found. Military service is a debt due to the Confederacy, and the power of exacting it should not depend on the accident of place. Conscription may be altogether avoided by large numbers of men, if merely crossing a line exonerates them from it. The practice of employing substitutes at pleasure, supposed to be authorized by the 9th section of the Conscript Act, has led to great abuses. The procuration of substitutes has become a regular business. Men thus obtained are usually unfit for service and frequently desert. The Department has restricted the practice by prohibiting the reception of unnaturalized foreigners as substitutes, but the evils of the system are still very great, and further restrictions are necessary.

It would be well to authorize substitution only where the services of the principal are equally useful to the public, at home as in the field. Such is the case with experts in trades necessary for the prosecution of the war, with overseers in districts of country having few whites and large numbers of slaves, and generally in such callings as are essential to the public welfare. It is unwise to injure the public service for the benefit of individuals, and therefore no substitution founded merely on considerations of private interest should be tolerated.

In this connection I desire to call attention to what seems to be an omission in the Exemption Act. Millers, tanners and saltmakers are essential to the prosecution of the war. Without them armies can neither be subsisted or properly clad. They are equally essential to the community at large, and the restriction of such callings to persons under eighteen and over thirty-five years of age inflict injury upon the army and upon the people. I recommend, therefore, that they be included in the Exemption Act.

The greatest defect in our present system is to be found in the rule of promotion established by the 10th section of the Conscript Act, and by the Acts of the Provisional Congress, approved December 11th, 1861, and January 22d, 1862. They require promotion to be by seniority. To this rule no valid objection could be made if provision were made for exceptional cases in which it becomes impracticable. In long established armies, seniority implies experience, and the rule is applied to individuals who, by previous examination or other test, have been found qualified for their position. In our armies there is little or no difference in the experience of our officers, and no test is applied to ascertain their moral or intellectual fitness for a commission.

As the act provides that commissions shall be granted by the President, it was supposed that this was intended as a safeguard against the admission of unqualified persons to important public trusts.

Accordingly, by General Order No. 39, a copy of which is herewith returned, Boards of Enquiry were directed to be summoned in all cases of promotion or election where the fitness of the claimant was doubtful. This, however, only keeps out unfit persons, but makes no provision for filling vacancies in case there be no unfit person in the corps, or in case all entitled to promotion decline it. Such cases occur and they contribute an element of disorganization and inefficiency in the army.

I earnestly recommend, therefore, that in all cases where election or promotion by seniority fails to fill a vacancy with a qualified officer, such vacancy may be filled by appointment. It may be objected that this increases executive patronage, and, by the intervention of examining boards, that promotion by seniority and by election may be cut off. If the increase of executive patronage be necessary to remove a great evil, its possible abuse is a poor argument against such increase. It is unwise to prefer certain evils to contingent abuses. Practically, it has been found difficult to get the examining boards to be rigid enough; they are too apt from indolence or good nature to scrutinize slightly the qualifications of brother officers, and would prove to be very unfit instruments for executive usurpation.

In this connection another serious difficulty in filling vacancies will be mentioned. It is generally supposed that the rule prescribed in the 10th section of the Conscript Act applies only to corps organized under that act; that the rule prescribed in the act approved December 11th, 1861, applies only to re-organizations of re-enlisted corps, very very few of which re-organizations actually took place, and that the act approved January 22d, 1862, applies only to troops raised under an act approved May 8th, 1861. But troops were authorized to be raised by acts approved May 11th, 1861, and August 8th, 1861, and questions arise as to what act troops come under, and what rule of promotion is provided for corps which come in under the act last mentioned. It is said that troops mustered directly into the Confederate States service receive their laws of promotion from Congress, and that those raised by the Governors of States, under requisition on them by the President, are governed by the laws of their respective States. It is maintained that the latter class are militia, and that, under the Constitution, Congress cannot provide for filling vacancies occurring in the militia.

Great confusion, uncertainty and inequality result from this state of things, and it is very important that a uniform rule should be applied to all. I know of no better rule than that already adopted, providing the power of appointment be given as recommended, and there be no constitutional impediments to its general application. A difficulty arises from the act authorizing the appointment of general officers which should be removed. The 6th section of the act approved March 6th, 1861, authorizes the President to organize Brigades and Divisions and to appoint commanding officers for them, who are to hold office only while such Brigades and Divisions are in service. If the casualties of service destroy a Brigade or a Division the commission of the General expires, and if separated from his command by ill health, wounds, or detached service, it is left without a head, there being no authority to appoint a successor without vacating the commission of the first appointee.

The army moreover requires the service of Generals not attached to Brigades and Divisions. There are certain duties which can be better performed by general officers than by officers of lower grade, but the merit requisite for the discharge of these duties secures promotion in the line, and officers of the line are therefore unwilling to surrender their positions for staff appointments. Brigades and Divisions are sometimes temporarily deprived of their commanders by the casualties of service, and it is desirable to assign general officers to such commands. It will be well, therefore, to increase the number of general officers to a definite excess above the whole number, not exceeding 8 or 10 per cent for the purposes above mentioned.

Congress, at its last session, authorized the appointment of eighty artillery officers for ordnance duties, the addition of fifty engineers to the provisional corps, and the organization of a signal corps, and a nitre corps.

All of these acts have been carried into execution. Eighty artillery officers for ordnance duty have been appointed and their duties prescribed and systematized. General Orders No. 24 and 46, herewith returned, require that every army corps shall have an ordnance officer with the rank of major, every division one with the rank of captain, every brigade one with the rank of first lieutenant, and every regiment an ordnance sergeant. These form a corps under the Chief of Ordnance at Richmond, to whom they are required to report. Their services are important for the proper distribution and preservation of arms. Ordnance officers are also required for arsenals. For the proper discharge of ordnance duties at arsenals, and in the field it will require a corps of at least one hundred and fifty.

I recommend, therefore, that application be made for the enlargement of the corps to that number, and that a limited number be authorized with the grade of major for service with army corps.

Most of the additional engineers have been appointed and the corps has done good service. The present law permits no higher grade than that of captain, while the other corps of the provisional army are organized in conformity with corresponding corps in the Confederate States army. This discrimination is unjust and impolitic. If men of talent and acquirement are needed in this corps, promotion should be offered equal to that attainable in other branches of the service.

Engineering talent is of a high order of endowment, and should be stimulated by proper rewards. I recommend, therefore, that the grade of the Provisional Engineer Corps should be made to conform to those of the same corps in the Confederate States army.

A Signal Corps has been organized by General Order No. 40, a copy of which is herewith returned. For the purpose of systematic instruction, a confidential pamphlet has been prepared by a member of the corps and printed with due precautions to avoid publicity. Should it, however, fall into the enemy's hands, no great harm would be done, as it contains the principles of the art merely, and does not disclose the key to any signal or cipher.

A Nitre Bureau has also been organized, and under its able and indefatigable head Major J. M. St. John, is doing good service. General Order No. 41, herewith communicated, was issued to facilitate the operations of the Bureau. The production of Nitre is already one thousand pounds a day, and there is good reason to think that it will reach three thousand pounds a day and supply our consumption.

A map of a reconnoisance, and Major St. John's report, are herewith returned. The Bureau has been directed to turn its attention to the mining of such materials as are required for the army, and will do much to develop their production.

The Act authorizing bands of Partizan Rangers has been carried into execution. Apprehending that the novelty of the organization, and the supposed freedom from control, would attract great numbers into the Partizan Corps, the department adopted a rule requiring a recommendation from a General commanding a department, before granting authority to raise partizans. Notwithstanding this restriction, there is reason to fear that the number of Partizan Corps greatly exceed the requirements of the service, and that they seriously impede recruiting for regiments of the line.

The precaution has been taken to require their organization to conform in all respects to that of other troops, and it will be only necessary to brigade such of them as are not needed for partizan service, to make them in fact, troops of the line, although nominally partizans. I recommend that this be authorized.

Since the adjournment of Congress, our stock of arms has been largely increased by importation and capture. Our small arms alone, have increased from these sources not less than eighty thousand. Our supply of ammunition has also been increased by importation and manufacture, and as already stated, we may expect at no distant day that the active and methodical operations of the Nitre Corps will supply our demand and make us independent of foreign importation.

I deem it unnecessary to say anything of the operations of the army since the adjournment of Congress. The time has not arrived for their complete disclosure, but enough has appeared to show the ability of our Generals and the courage and patience of our troops.

It is to be regretted that we cannot reward such services as the army has rendered, they are infinitely above all compensation, but something may be done to show our appreciation of them. Courage and skill cannot always command promotion. Happily for us, they far exceed our means of reward, if confined to mere material benefits. It would, however, be doing our high-toned soldiers great injustice to suppose that rank and pay are their only incentives to exertion. I think that medals conferred as rewards for good conduct in the field, cultivate the spirit which distinguishes the patriot soldier from the mercenary, and afford means of reward without injuring the army by excessive promotion.

I recommend, therefore, that application be made for authority to confer medals upon such officers and men as distinguish themselves in battle.

A right to control the operations of our Railroads to some extent, is necessary to insure quick and safe transportation, and to maintain the roads in a proper state of efficiency. The regular transportation of the roads is so much deranged by the movements of troops and munitions of war, that a common head during the war is indispensable. I recommend that application be for authority to exercise such control as may be necessary to harmonize the operations of the roads, and to maintain their efficiency, and to appoint a Superintendent, who shall be charged with the supervision of Railroad transportation.

           Very respectfully,

              Your obedient servant,

                  GEO. W. RANDOLPH,

                      Secretary of War.

WAR DEPARTMENT,
ADJUTANT AND INSPECTOR GENERAL'S OFFICE,
Richmond, April 28, 1862.

GENERAL ORDERS, }
No. 30. }

I. The following acts having passed both Houses of Congress, were duly approved by the President, and are now published for the information of the army:

AN ACT TO ORGANIZE BANDS OF PARTIZAN RANGERS.

SEC. 1. *The Congress of the Confederate States of America do enact,* That the President be and he is hereby authorized to commission such officers as he may deem proper, with authority to form bands of Partizan Rangers, in companies, battalions or regiments, either as infantry or cavalry, the companies, battalions or regiments to be composed, each, of such numbers as the President may approve.

SEC. 2. *Be it further enacted,* That such Partizan Rangers, after being regularly received into the service, shall be entitled to the same pay, rations and quarters, during their term of service, and be subject to the same regulations as other soldiers.

SEC. 3. *Be it further enacted,* That for any arms and munitions of war captured from the enemy by any body of Partizan Rangers, and delivered to any quartermaster at such place or places as may be designated by a Commanding General, the Rangers shall be paid their full value, in such manner as the Secretary of War may prescribe.

Approved April 21, 1862.

AN ACT TO FURTHER PROVIDE FOR THE PUBLIC DEFENCE.

In view of the exigencies of the country, and the absolute necessity of keeping in the service our gallant army, and of placing in the field a large additional force to meet the advancing columns of the enemy now invading our soil: Therefore,

SEC. 1. *The Congress of the Confederate States of America do enact,* That the President be and he is hereby authorized to call out and place in the military service of the Confederate States, for three years, unless the war shall have been sooner ended, all white men who are residents of the Confederate States, between the ages of eighteen and thirty-five years at the time the call or calls may be made, who are legally exempted from military service. All of the persons aforesaid who are now in the armies of the Confederacy, and whose term of service will expire before the end of the war, shall be continued in the service for three years from the date of their original enlistment, unless the war shall have been sooner ended: *Provided, however,* That all such companies, squadrons, battalions and regiments, whose term of original enlistment was for twelve months, shall have the right, within forty days, on a day to be fixed by the commander of the brigade, to reorganize said companies, battalions and regiments, by electing all their officers which they had a right heretofore to elect, who shall be commissioned by the President: *Provided further,* That furloughs not exceeding sixty days, with transportation home and back, shall be granted to all those retained in the service by the provisions of this act, beyond the period of their original enlistment, and who have not heretofore received furloughs under the provisions of an act entitled "An Act providing for the granting of bounty and furloughs to privates and non-commissioned officers in the Provisional Army," approved 11th December, eighteen hundred and sixty one; said furloughs to be granted at such times and in such numbers as the Secretary of War may deem most compatible with the public interest: *And provided further,* That in lieu of a furlough, the commutation value in money of the transportation herein above granted, shall be paid to each private, musician or non-commissioned officer who may elect to receive it, at such time as the furlough would otherwise be granted: *Provided further,* That all persons under the age of eighteen years or over the age of thirty-five years, who are now enrolled in the military service of the Confederate States, in the regiments, squadrons, battalions and companies hereafter to be reorganized, shall be required to remain in their respective companies, squadrons, battalions and regiments for ninety days, unless their places can be sooner supplied by other recruits not now in the service, who are between the ages of eighteen and thirty-five years: and all laws and parts of laws providing for the re-enlistment of volunteers and the organization thereof into companies, squadrons, battalions or regiments, shall be and the same are hereby repealed.

SEC. 2. *Be it further enacted,* That such companies, squadrons, battalions or regiments organized, or in process of organization by authority from the Secretary of War, as may be within thirty days from the passage of this act, so far completed as to have the whole number of men requisite for organization actually enrolled, not embracing in said organization any persons now in service, shall be mustered into the service of the Confederate States as part of the land forces of the same; to be received in that arm of the service in which they are authorized to organize; and shall elect their company, battalion and regimental officers.

SEC. 3. *Be it further enacted,* That for the enrollment of all persons comprehended within the provisions of this act, who are not already in service in the armies of the Confederate States, it shall be lawful for the President, with the consent of the governors of the respective States, to employ State officers; and on failure to obtain such consent, he shall employ Confederate officers, charged with the duty of making such enrollment in accordance with rules and regulations to be prescribed by him.

SEC. 4. *Be it further enacted,* That persons enrolled under the provisions of the preceding section, shall be assigned by the Secretary of War to the different companies now in service, until each company is filled to its maximum number, and the persons so enrolled shall be assigned to companies from the States from which they respectively come.

Sec. 5. *Be it further enacted,* That all seamen and ordinary seamen in the land forces of the Confederate States, enrolled under the provisions of this act, may, on application of the Secretary of the Navy, be transferred from the land forces to the naval service.

Sec. 6. *Be it further enacted,* That in all cases where a State may not have in the army a number of regiments, battalions, squadrons or companies sufficient to absorb the number of persons subject to military service under this act, belonging to such State, then the residue or excess thereof shall be kept as a reserve, under such regulations as may be established by the Secretary of War, and that at stated periods of not greater than three months, details, determined by lot, shall be made from said reserve, so that each company shall, as nearly as practicable, be kept full : *Provided,* That the persons held in reserve may remain at home until called into service by the President: *Provided also,* That during their stay at home, they shall not receive pay : *Provided further,* That the persons comprehended in this act shall not be subject to the Rules and Articles of War until mustered into the actual service of the Confederate States; except that said persons, when enrolled and liable to duty, if they shall wilfully refuse to obey said call, each of them shall be held to be a deserter, and punished as such, under said articles: *Provided further,* That whenever, in the opinion of the President, the exigencies of the public service may require it, he shall be authorized to call into actual service the entire reserve, or so much as may be necessary, not previously assigned to different companies in service under provision of section four of this act. Said reserve shall be organized under such rules as the Secretary of War may adopt : *Provided,* The company, battalion and regimental officers shall be elected by the troops composing the same : *Provided,* The troops raised in any one State shall not be combined in regimental, battalion, squadron or company organization with troops raised in any other States.

Sec. 7. *Be it further enacted,* That all soldiers now serving in the army or mustered in the military service of the Confederate States, or enrolled in said service under the authorizations heretofore issued by the Secretary of War, and who are continued in the service by virtue of this act, who have not received the bounty of fifty dollars allowed by existing laws, shall be entitled to receive said bounty.

Sec. 8. *Be it further enacted,* That each man who may hereafter be mustered into the service, and who shall arm himself with a musket, shot-gun, rifle or carbine, accepted as an efficient weapon, shall be paid the value thereof, to be ascertained by the mustering officer, under such regulations as may be prescribed by the Secretary of War, if he is willing to sell the same ; and if he is not, then he shall be entitled to receive one dollar a month for the use of said received and approved musket, rifle, shot-gun or carbine.

SEC. 9. *Be it further enacted*, That persons not liable for duty may be received as substitutes for those who are, under such regulations as may be prescribed by the Secretary of War.

SEC. 10. *Be it further enacted*, That all vacancies shall be filled by the President from the company, battalion, squadron or regiment in which such vacancies shall occur, by promotion according to seniority, except in cases of disability or other incompetency : *provided, however*, that the President may, when in his opinion it may be proper, fill such vacancy or vacancies by the promotion of any officer or officers, or private or privates from such company, battalion, squadron or regiment who shall have been distinguished in the service by exhibition of valor and skill, and that whenever a vacancy shall occur in the lowest grade of the commissioned officers of a company, said vacancy shall be filled by election : *provided*, that all appointments made by the President shall be by and with the advice and consent of the Senate.

SEC. 11. *Be it further enacted*, That the provisions of the first section of this act relating to the election of officers, shall apply to those regiments, battalions, and squadrons which are composed of twelve months and war companies combined in the same organization, without regard to the manner in which the officers thereof were originally appointed.

SEC. 12. *Be it further enacted*, That each company of infantry shall consist of one hundred and twenty-five, rank and file ; each company of field artillery of one hundred and fifty, rank and file ; and each of cavalry, of eighty, rank and file.

SEC. 13. *Be it further enacted*, That all persons subject to enrollment, who are not now in the service, under the provisions of this act, shall be permitted, previous to such enrollment, to volunteer in companies now in the service. [Approved April 16th, 1862.]

II. ENROLLMENT AND DISPOSITION OF RECRUITS.

1. An officer not below the rank of Major, will be detailed for each State, to take charge of the enrollment, mustering in, subsistence, transportation and disposition of the Recruits raised under the above act.

2. Application will be made immediately to the Governors of the several States, for permission to employ State officers for said enrollment ; and in case such permission be not granted, officers of the army will be selected by the Department to perform that duty, under such regulations as may be prescribed. Where State officers are employed, the regulations of the respective States in regard to military enrollment, will be observed as far as applicable.

3. The enrolled men in each State will be collected in camps of instruction, by the officers in command of the Recruits, the said camps to be selected with reference to health, and the facilities for obtaining subsistence and transportation. The number of these camps shall not exceed two in each State, without authority from the Department ; and to each will be allowed a Quartermaster and a Commissary.

4. The commandants of the camps of instruction in the several States will call upon the Generals commanding the military depart-

ments in which their camps may be situated, for competent drill officers to instruct the recruits, and will prepare them for the field as rapidly as possible. They will cause them to be promptly vaccinated; and in ordering them to the field, will, as far as practicable, prefer those who have passed through the usual camp diseases. They will establish hospitals in connection with their camps, and make requisition for such medical attendance and stores as may be required.

5. The commandants of regiments, battalions, squadrons and unattached companies in service on the 16th instant, will send copies of their muster rolls to the commandant of the proper camp of instruction in their respective States, with officers to take charge of such recruits as may be furnished to said corps. The said commandants will apportion the recruits among such corps, in proportion to the deficiency of each, except when otherwise specially directed by the Department, allotting as far as practicable to each such corps the men from the regions of country in which it has been raised. They will from time to time send off such bodies of recruits as are ready for the field, and will report on the first Monday of every month to the Department, the number of recruits in camp, their condition, the number sent off during the month, and the regiments and corps to which they were sent.

6. The commandants of regiments and corps will distribute the recruits among their several companies; and in such as have not the number of companies allowed by law to a regiment, the said commandants may organize the required number of new companies, after first filling up the existing companies to the minimum numbers required by law; that is to say, for each company of infantry, 64 privates; of cavalry, 60 privates; of artillery, 70 privates.

7. The recruits will be apportioned among the several arms of service, according to their respective wants, consulting as far as practicable, the preference of the men. Where a greater number offer for a particular arm than can be assigned to it, the distribution will be determined by lot; but recruits for the cavalry will only be taken from those who furnish their own horses.

III. Volunteers for Existing Corps.

8. Persons liable to military service under the above act, not in service on the 16th of April, and wishing to volunteer in any particular company in the Confederate service on the 16th day of April, may report themselves prior to their enrollment, at a camp of instruction within their respective States, where they will be enrolled, prepared for the field, and sent to the said company, until the s me shall be filled up.

9. Recruiting officers may be detailed, with the permission of the Generals commanding military departments, by the commandants of regiments and corps, and sent to their respective States for the purpose of receiving for such regiments and corps, in conformity with recruiting regulations heretofore adopted (General Orders, No. 6), all volunteers desiring to join them. Such volunteers may be assembled at the camps of instruction in their respective States, prepared for the field, and sent

to their respective regiments and corps, until the same shall be filled up; or, if ready for the field, may be ordered directly to their corps by the officer so recruiting them.

IV.—VOLUNTEER CORPS HERETOFORE AUTHORIZED.

10. Persons liable to military service under this act, and not in service on the 16th day of April, may, until the 17th day of May next, volunteer in corps heretofore authorized to be raised by the Secretary of War, or by the Executive of any State, as part of the quota thereof, in pursuance of a call made upon such State by the President. Persons authorized to raise such corps, who may not on that day have the necessary number of men enrolled and mustered into service, according to the terms of their authority, will proceed with their men to a camp of instruction in their respective States, and will deliver their muster rolls to the commandant thereof.

11. The commandants of such corps as are completed on or before the 17th day of May, and not otherwise ordered, will report to the commandants of the recruits of their respective States, and with their corps will be placed by him in a camp of instruction, and reported immediately to the Department. Such corps will be under the command of the commandants of recruits in their respective States, and will be prepared for the field in like manner with the recruits, until removed from the camp. They will only be moved under orders from the Department, from the Commanding General of the army, or in urgent cases, from the Commanding General of the military department in which the camps may be situated; and in such cases, report will immediately be made to the Department by the officer in command of the camp.

V.—ADDITIONAL CORPS. GUERRILLA SERVICE.

12. Under the prohibition of this act against the organization of new corps, no further authority for that purpose can be given, except that specially provided for in the act of Congress, entitled "an act to organize bands of Partizan Rangers." For this latter purpose, applications must be made through the Commanding Generals of the military departments in which the said corps are to be employed.

VI.—REORGANIZATION OF TWELVE MONTHS CORPS.

13. All regiments, battalions, squadrons and companies of 12 months volunteers will reorganize within 40 days from the 16th of April, by electing all their officers which they had a right heretofore to elect, and on such days as the brigade commander may prescribe; and the said brigade commanders are hereby ordered to fix and announce the day for such reorganization as soon as practicable. No person who is to be discharged under the provisions of the act, will take part in such election.

14. The form of holding and certifying the elections will be in conformity with the laws of the State from which the men, or the major part thereof, may come; and when the election of field officers is to be made by company officers, the latter will be first elected. All certificates of election will be returned to the Adjutant General's office, and the officers will be commissioned by the President. They will, however, on receiving a copy of the certificate of election, immediately enter upon duty. Officers not re-elected will be relieved from duty, and the brigade commander will return their names to the Department.

VII.—Corps raised for Local Defence.

15. Corps raised for local defence will retain their organization during the term of such enlistment, unless previously disbanded; but members of such corps may volunteer into corps for general service, as herein above provided.

VIII.—Discharges.

16. When any company now in service for 12 months shall, before the 16th day of July next, attain the maximum numbers prescribed by this act, without including the men under 18 and over 35 years of age, all such men may be discharged, and such of them as remain in service on the said day will, upon their application, be then discharged, whether such maximum be attained or not.

IX.—Transfers.

17. The right to change company or corps in virtue of re-enlistment, ceases to exist by the repeal of all laws in regard to re-enlistment; but transfers of individuals or of companies may be made, as heretofore, within the discretion of the Department, on applications approved by commanding officers.

X.—Substitutes.

18. When any person liable to military duty under this act, but not yet mustered into service in any company, desires to furnish a substitute, he shall report himself with the substitute to the commandant of a camp of instruction; and if the substitute be lawfully exempt from military duty, and on examination by a Surgeon or Assistant Surgeon, be pronounced sound and in all respects fit for military service, he may be accepted and enrolled; and the person furnishing such substitute may be discharged by the commandant of the camp. But no substitute shall be entitled to transportation or other allowance at the expense of the Government, until so accepted and enrolled.

XI.—Exemptions.

19. Persons claiming exemption from military duty under this act, shall be required by the enrolling officer to make oath that they are lawfully exempt, and shall be furnished by him with a certificate of such exemption.

By command of the Secretary of War.

S. COOPER,
Adjutant and Inspector General.

GENERAL ORDERS, ⎰
No. 39.　　　⎱

I. The second paragraph of General Orders, No. 36, is hereby revoked, and the following substituted therefor : When an officer elected or promoted in the provisional army by reason of seniority, is by law to be commissioned by the President, and there is reasonable ground to doubt his qualification or fitness for the commission, his brigade commander, if there be one, or if not, then his division commander will assemble a board of not less than three commissioned officers of equal or superior rank to the officer elected or promoted, who shall enquire into his qualifications and fitness for the commission, and shall report to this office, for the information of the War Department, the facts of the case, and their own opinion of the qualification and fitness of the officer. This order will apply to all persons not yet commissioned or recognized as in commission by the Department.

II. The limits of Department No. 1, under command of Major General Lovell, will hereafter embrace that portion of the State of Mississippi south of the 33d parallel and west of Pascagoula and Chickasawha rivers, including also that part of the State of Louisiana east of the Mississippi river.

III. Department No. 2, under command of General Beauregard, is extended south to the 33d parallel east of the Tennessee river, and extending on that parallel to the eastern boundary of Alabama

IV. The boundary of the Trans-Mississippi Department will embrace the States of Missouri and Arkansas, including the Indian Territory, the State of Louisiana west of the Mississippi, and the State of Texas.

V. Frequent complaints having been made of injury to fencing and to the grounds on or near which troops have encamped, attention is called to the 983d paragraph of the Army Regulations, which requires the Commanding Officer and Quarter Master to make an inspection of buildings occupied as barracks, quarters, or lands occupied for encampments, when they are vacated, and a report to be made to the Quarter Master General of their condition, and of any injury to them by the use of the troops.

This regulation will be strictly enforced ; and in case of injury not reported by the Commanding Officer and Quarter Master, they will be charged on their pay account of the troops with the damage done. If report be made, it must specify by whom the injury was inflicted, and the deduction, in such case, will be made from the pay of the offending party.

I. Hereafter Brigadier Generals will have timely requisitions made for all blanks issued from this office, in order that they may be forwarded for early distribution.

By command of the Secretary of War.

S. COOPER,

Adjutant and Inspector General.

GENERAL ORDERS, }
No. 24. }

I. All officers assigned to ordnance duty with troops in the field, will be reported to the Adjutant and Inspector General of the Army, and will report by letter to the Chief of the Ordnance. Bureau in Richmond.

II. Every General in command of an Army Corps will, if no officer is assigned to his Army for the purpose, designate an officer for ordnance duty, as "Chief of Ordnance" of that Army, who shall, while on such duty, if of inferior grade in the Confederate Army, be entitled to the rank and pay of a Major of Artillery.

III. Every Major General in command of a division, or Brigadier General, whose brigade constitutes a separate command, will, under like circumstances, designate an officer for ordnance duty, as "Division Ordnance Officer" (or "Brigade Ordnance Officer," if the brigade constitutes a separate command,) who shall, if a subaltern in the Confederate Army, have the rank and pay of a Captain of Artillery.

IV. Officers so appointed shall be selected on account of fitness for ordnance duties, and shall be considered as attached to the Ordnance Bureau, and will not be changed, except by authority obtained from the Head Quarters of the Army, through the Chief of the Bureau of Ordnance.

V. Every commanding officer of a Regiment will select from the non-commissioned officers of the Regiment the one best qualified for the duty of Ordnance Sergeant, and will appoint him Acting Ordnance Sergeant. Such non-commissioned officer will have charge of all the surplus Ordnance Stores of the Regiment, and will make returns of the same to the Ordnance Bureau. The arms and accoutrements of the sick and disabled of the Regiment will be turned over to and be accounted for by him. He will exercise supervision over the arms and ammunition in the hands of the men, and report any waste or damage to the Division Ordnance officer, through the Colonel of the Regiment. All such appointments will be reported through the General Head Quarters, to the Chief of the Ordnance Bureau.

VI. The "Chief of Ordnance" of an Army, will require reports monthly, or oftener, from "Division Ordnance Officers," and will be responsible for the supply of Ordnance and Ordnance Stores with the Army to which he is attached.

VII. The Division Ordnance Officers will make reports monthly, or oftener, if required, to the "Chief of Ordnance" of the Army to which the division belongs. They will be responsible for all Ordnance Stores with the division—not in the hands of the troops—and make returns thereof to the Bureau of Ordnance.

VIII. Chiefs of Ordnance of Armies and all Ordnance Officers in the field are attached to the staffs of their respective commands, but will nevertheless conform to such orders and instructions received from the Chief of the Bureau of Ordnance in relation to the execution of their appropriate duties as do not interfere with the orders of the commanding officers in the field.

IX. It is especially enjoined on all Officers of Ordnance to prevent waste of small arms and field ammunition in the hands of troops, and to cause unserviceable ammunition to be sent off to the nearest Ordnance Depot. Arms, accoutrements and equipments which cannot be repaired in the field, will in like manner be forwarded for immediate repairs.

X. Ordnance Officers serving on the staff of Generals commanding, will not enter into contracts for, or purchase Ordnance Supplies, except in case of necessity, on the authority of the General; which must be attached to the contract, or account for such purchase. The exigency requiring the contract or purchase, will also be stated therein.

By command of the Secretary of War.

S. COOPER,
Adjutant and Inspector General.

GENERAL ORDERS, ⎰
No. 46. ⎱

I. The following Regulations are published for the information of the Army:

1. Paragraph III, General Orders No. 24, current series, is so modified as to permit the appointment of Brigade Ordnance Officers, who shall have the rank and pay of First Lieutenants of Artillery.

2. Brigade Ordnance Officers so appointed will be subject to the Division Ordnance Officers, so far as relates to ordnance duties, and will make requisitions on them. They will also make such reports as may be required, to the Division Ordnance Officers.

3. Ordnance Sergeants of Regiments will be subject to, and make reports to the Brigade Ordnance Officers.

4. Since the Act of April 19, 1862, providing an Ordnance Sergeant to each Regiment, the acting appointees, authorized under General Orders No. 24, current series, and made by Colonels of Regiments, will be reported for appointment under the above act, in cases where such report has not been made to the Ordnance Bureau. Hereafter the appointments will be made to Regiments as to Military Posts, by the Secretary of War, and upon 'the recommendation of Colonels of Regiments, through the Ordnance Bureau, the non-commissioned officers recommended being at once placed upon duty in anticipation of the appointment.

II. Paragraph IV, Generals Orders No. 44, current series, is hereby rescinded, and the following paragraph is substituted in lieu thereof:

Persons under 18 and over 35 years of age, who have re-enlisted for three years or the war, are not entitled to their discharge under the Conscript Act. Persons of the ages above mentioned, who enlisted for twelve months, or for a shorter term, will be entitled to their discharge ninety days after the expiration of their term of service.

III. All Chaplains taken prisoners of war by the Armies of the Confederate States, while engaged in the discharge of their proper duties, will be immediately and unconditionally released.

By command of the Secretary of War.

S. COOPER,
Adjutant and Inspector General.

GENERAL ORDERS, }
No. 41. }

I. General officers and officers in command of departments, districts and separate posts, will make a detail of men from their commands to work the Nitre Caves, which may be situated within the limits of their respective commands. These details will be made on the requisition of the officer in charge of the Nitre Bureau in the War Department. The men thus detailed will be organized temporarily under the command of the Nitre officer in charge of the particular cave, who will make monthly reports to the general or other officer commanding the department, district or post in which the cave may be located, in order that such commanding officer may treat as deserters such of the detailed men as may leave the works without permission. And it is enjoined upon Generals and other commanding officers to give protection, as far as possible, and to the extent of their means, against any encroachments of the enemy upon the Nitre Caves within the limits of their commands.

II. All persons in the employment of the Nitre Bureau, whether contractors for manufacturing saltpetre, or laborers in their employment, are exempt by law from enrollment.

III. Officers of the Quartermaster and Commissary Departments will furnish the officers and men of the Nitre Bureau with provision and forage as in the case of ordnance officers and men in the field.

IV. Officers of the Nitre Bureau are authorized to impress free negroes for the purpose of working the Nitre Caves, who will be paid wages and be furnished with subsistence.

V. Paragraph No. 161, General Regulations of the Army, relating to Discharges in Hospital, is so far modified as to dispense with the necessity of sending certificates of disability in the case of soldiers sick in the hospitals in Richmond, to the commandants of regiments, where communication with them is difficult and the cases urgent. In all such cases, the certificates will be sent to Brigadier-General John H. Winder, commanding the Department of Henrico, who will grant the Discharge, and notify the same to the Regimental Commander, who will cause the final statements in each case of discharge to be made out and sent to the officer granting the discharge, for the benefit of the discharged soldier.

VI. The following is published for the information of all concerned:
The act No. 52, approved March 6, 1861, section 19, provides, " that there shall be allowed, in addition to the pay herein before provided, to every commissioned officer, except the Surgeon General, nine

dollars per month for every five years' service; and to the officers of the army of the United States, who have resigned, or may resign, to be received into the service of the Confederate States, this additional pay shall be allowed from the date of their entrance into the former service."

The foregoing act applies to all officers of the United States army, who have resigned from that army, to be received into the service of the Confederate States, whether in the regular or provisional army.

By command of the Secretary of War.

S. COOPER,
Adjutant and Inspector General.

WAR DEPARTMENT,

ADJUTANT AND INSPECTOR GENERAL'S OFFICE,
Richmond, May 29, 1862.

GENERAL ORDERS, }
    No. 40. }

I. The following Act of Congress and Regulations in reference thereto, are published for the information of the Army, viz:

AN ACT TO ORGANIZE A SIGNAL CORPS.

SEC. 1. *The Congress of the Confederate States of America do enact,* That the President be and is hereby authorized, by and with the advice and consent of the Senate, to appoint ten officers in the Provisional Army, of a grade not exceeding that of Captains, and with the pay of corresponding grades of infantry, who shall perform the duties of signal officers of the army. And the President is hereby authorized to appoint ten Sergeants of Infantry in the Provisional Army, and to assign them to duty as Signal Sergeants. The signal corps above authorized may be organized as a separate corps, or may be attached to the department of the Adjutant and Inspector General, or to the Engineer Corps, as the Secretary of War shall direct.

[Approved April 19, 1862.]

II. The Signal Corps authorized by this act will be attached to the Adjutant and Inspector General's department; and officers of that department may be instructed in and assigned to signal duty.

III. A signal officer will be attached to the staff of each General or Major General in command of a corps, and of each Major General in command of a division. These signal officers will each be assisted by as many Signal Sergeants, and instructed non-commissioned officers and privates, selected from the ranks for their intelligence and reliability, as circumstances may require; and as many Lance Sergeants as are required may be appointed. Such non-commissioned officers and privates may be detailed for this duty by the Generals in whose command they are serving. Before being instructed, they will each be required by the signal officer to take an oath not to divulge, directly or indirectly, the system of signals, the alphabet, or any official message sent or received thereby. Non-commissioned officers, while on signal duty, and privates on this duty, will receive 40 cents per day extra pay.

IV. Commissioned officers of the Signal Corps, or officers serving on signal duty, will be entitled to the forage and allowance of officers of similar rank in the cavalry. Non-commissioned officers and privates on signal duty will be mounted by the Quartermaster, on the order of the Commanding General.

V. Requisitions for flags, torches, glasses, and all the material required, will be made on the Quartermaster's department, or they may be purchased by the Quartermaster of any division, on the order of the Major General commanding.

VI. On the order of the General commanding a corps, other officers, non-commissioned officers or privates than those regularly on signal duty, may be instructed in the system of signals, after having taken the oath prescribed above. Wherever it is practicable, it is specially recommended to all general officers to have their Assistant Adjutant Generals and Aid de Camps instructed.

VII. Whatever is prescribed herein for a division, or for a Major General, will be observed in the case of each brigade which constitutes a separate command.

VIII. All officers and non-commissioned officers accepting appointments to the Signal Corps, will forward with their acceptances the oath prescribed above, sworn to before a magistrate, notary public, or commissioned officer of the corps.

IX. Quarterly returns of signal property will be made by all officers having it in charge, to the Quartermaster's department, and the senior signal officer of each separate army in the field will report quarterly to the Adjutant and Inspector General the number and organization of the Signal Corps of the Army, and its general operations during the previous quarter.

X. It will be the duty of the signal officer of every division in the field to instruct the Adjutant of each regiment in the division in the system of signals in use in the army.

By command of the Secretary of War.

S. COOPER,
Adjutant and Inspector General.

POSTOFFICE DEPARTMENT,
Richmond, August 18, 1862.

Sir: At the opening of the last session of Congress, I made a very full report of the operations of the Postoffice Department. The short time which has elapsed since the making of that report does not furnish data on which an extended report need now be made. I shall, therefore, limit this report to such matters as have since arisen, and upon which information may be desired.

The surrender of New Orleans and Memphis, and the occupation of the Mississippi River by the Federal forces, have very seriously interrupted the regularity and usefulness of the mails along that river, and in the States of Arkansas, Louisiana and Texas; and this, with the occupation by the Federal forces of the greater portion of the State of Tennessee, and other localities, must have greatly reduced the revenues of the Department—though sufficient time has not elapsed to enable the auditor to receive the returns and report the amount of decrease of revenue growing out of these causes.

After the fall of New Orleans, and before the Mississippi River was occupied at and below Memphis, anticipating the embarrassments likely to arise from the occupation of that river by the enemy, I prepared and forwarded full and detailed instructions to D. P. Blair, Hugh Francis and J. E. Talbot, special agents of this Department, requiring them, in case the river should be so occupied, to ascertain the best routes and means of conveying the mails across the river and swamps, and empowered them to employ messengers to carry the mails by any routes and by any modes of conveyance which could be made available. And they were instructed to devote their personal attention to these duties. Special Agent Blair has performed his duties with great activity and efficiency.

The overflow of the railroads leading westward from Memphis and Vicksburg, which were the great arteries through which the mails for Arkansas and Northern Louisiana, and a large portion of Texas are supplied, had produced serious delays and difficulties in the way of a regular transmission of the mails prior to the occupation of those points by the enemy. The river bottoms remained overflowed for some time subsequent to the occupation of the main points upon the river, and aided in rendering the postal communication slow and uncertain.

The postal communication across the Mississippi River is somewhat improved and more reliable; though it cannot become satisfactory until we regain control of that river.

New lines of communication have been established across the swampy and sparsely settled country bordering on the Mississippi, through which even the minor local mails have not heretofore been carried, (the offices having been supplied chiefly by the river route from New Orleans;) and the condition of the new routes and uncertainty of securing a safe passage across the river, have added greatly to the difficulties which the Department is required to overcome.

The proposals for contracts for mail service in Arkansas, Texas and Louisiana (together with other States) for four years from the first of July last, were required by the terms of the advertisement, to be decided by the 31st May, 1862; and anticipating difficulty in giving to the successful bidders timely notice of the acceptance of their proposals, I retained in this city a special agent of the Department, for the purpose of sending the notices of acceptance across the Mississippi river by him, to be mailed at the nearest office on the other side. The difficulties before referred to prevented the receipt of the notices, in numerous cases, in time to enable the new contractors to stock the routes and begin service on the 1st July. This delay produced some confusion in the mail service, which was partially overcome by postmasters obtaining, temporarily, the services of the old contractors.

In addition to the States above named, proposals for new service were received from the States of Mississippi, Alabama and Tennessee, for the contract term of four years; and it is found that the cost of the service in all of these States, has been greatly increased, by the causes suggested in my last report as likely to produce such a result.

The act approved April 19th, 1862, establishing a uniform rate of postage of ten cents on single letters, and the act approved April 21st, reducing the amount of commission allowed to postmasters, have not been in operation long enough to enable me to determine their effect upon the revenues of the Department.

The receipts and expenditures of the Postoffice Department, for the three quarters for which the accounts have been made up in the Auditor's office and for the fractional part of a quarter, embracing the month of June, 1861, are as follows:

For the quarter which ended September 30th, 1861, embracing the preceding month of June,

The expenditures were,	-	-	-	668,727 34
Receipts,	-	-		414,163 64
Excess of expenditures,		-	-	$254,563 70

For the quarter which ended December 31st, 1861,

The expenditures were,	-	-		721,430 29
Receipts,	-	-	-	491,163 64
Excess of expenditures,	-	-		$230,266 65

For the quarter which ended March 31st, 1862,

The expenditures were,	-	-		674,218 77
Receipts,	-	-	-	418,802 52
Excess of expenditures,	-		-	$255,416 25

The aggregate expenditures for the ten months, which ended 31st March, 1862, were	-		2,064,376 40
Aggregate receipts,	-	-	1,324,121 90
Aggregate excess of expenditures,		-	$740,254 50

It is to be borne in mind, that the expenditures as shown above, were incurred under the contracts made with the government of the United States, and before the reductions of the cost of service by the reduction and discontinuance of the service made by this Department, had gone into operation. The reductions of the cost of the service by the various means set forth in my last report, will probably show a considerable decrease of expenditure for the quarter which ended June 30th, 1862. And both the receipts and expenditures of the Department will be materially reduced for that and the succeeding quarters, by the occupation of portions of our territory by the enemy and the interruption of our postal communication across the Mississippi river. The increased cost of the service under the new contracts referred to in a previous part of this report, will tend to prevent the Department from becoming self-supporting by the time prescribed by the Constitution. It remains to be seen whether the increase of the rates of postage, the reduction of the commissions heretofore paid to postmasters, and the reduction of the cost of service by the various means mentioned in my last report, will furnish a revenue equal to the current expenditures of the Department. That it would have done so, if we could have held all our territory free from the occupation of the enemy, I have little doubt.

If the measures already adopted by Congress and by this Department fail to make its revenues equal to its expenditures, by the time prescribed by the Constitution, a still further reduction of the cost of the service, and consequently of postal facilities, must necessarily follow, unless it be deemed advisable by Congress to make a still greater increase of the rates of postage. And this latter alternative would be of doubtful policy, unless rendered expedient by the increased amount of currency in circulation and the consequent enhancement of the cost of the service, as of everything else. It may be doubtful, even in view of such a condition of things, whether the revenues of the Department would be increased by an increase of the rates of postage.

To show the difference between the receipts and expenditures of the postal service, for the first ten months under the Government of the Confederate States and for a like period of time under the Government of the United States, the following figures are presented:

The expenditures under the Government of the United States for the ten months which ended June 30th, 1860, were - -	$3,580,205 66
Expenditures under the Government of the Confederate States for the ten months which ended March 31st, 1862, -	2,064,376 40
Showing a reduction in the cost of the service for that period of - - -	1,515,829 26
The receipts for that period under the Government of the United States were -	1,264,200 47
Receipts for the same period under the Government of the Confederate States, -	1,324,121 90
Showing an increase of receipts under the Confederate Government of - -	59,921 43

From this it will be seen that the cost of the service has been greatly reduced, and that there has been a small increase of the revenues of the Department.

I renew the suggestions of my last report in favor of the payment of mail contractors for the services performed by them after their several States seceded from the Government of the United States, and before the Government of the Confederate States took control of the service.

I am, with great respect,

Your obedient servant,

JOHN H. REAGAN,

Postmaster General.

To the President.

MESSAGE OF THE PRESIDENT.

RICHMOND, VA. Aug. 19, 1862.

To the Senate and House of Representatives of the Confederate States :

I herewith transmit for your information the report of the Secretary of the Treasury and accompanying estimates, to which reference was made in my message of yesterday, and invite your careful attention to the statements and recommendations contained in them.

JEFFERSON DAVIS.

REPORT OF THE SECRETARY OF THE TREASURY·

TREASURY DEPARTMENT, C. S. A.,

Richmond, *August 18th*, 1862.

Hon. Thomas S. Bocock,

Speaker of House of Representatives, C. S. A. :

Sir : I have the honor to submit the following report of the condition of this Department, and of the estimates and supplies requisite for the support of the Government, until the 1st of January ensuing :

The receipts at the Treasury up to 1st August from all the various sources of income are as follows :

From Customs,	$1,437,399 96
" Miscellaneous sources,	1,974,769 33
" Loan, act of Feb. 28th, 1861,	15,000,000 00
" do " Aug. 19th, 1861,	22,613,346 61
" call Deposits under act of December 24th, 1861,	37,585,200 00
" Treasury Notes, act March 9th, 1861,	2,021,100 00
" do do " May 16th, 1861,	17,347,955 00
" do do " Aug. 19th, 1861,	167,764,615 00
" Int. do do " April 17th, 1861,	22,799,900 00
" 1 & $2 do do "	846,000 00
" Temporary Loan from banks—balance,	2,625,000 00
" War Tax,	10,539,910 70
	$302,555,196 60

The expenditures at the same date are as follows :

War Department,	$298,376,549 41
Navy Department,	14,605,777 86
Civil and Miscellaneous,	15,766,503 43
	$328,748,830 70

The difference between this sum and the receipts, amounting to $26,193,634 10 is made up of the various balances on the books of the Treasury to the credit of disbursing officers, which are not yet paid.

There are, also, outstanding requisitions upon the Treasury, upon which warrants are not yet issued, as follows :

48

War Department,	-	-	-	-	$ 18,112,192 15
Navy do	-	-	-	-	411,936 00

$18,524,128 15

This sum must be added to the expenditures paid as above, in order to exhibit the whole expenditures of the Government from its commencement to the 1st August, and the aggregate is $ 347,272,958 85, and for still greater accuracy it should be stated that as about five millions of the amount charged as expenditure has been paid for the redemption of Deposit Certificates, the aggregate above stated is subject to that abatement, when considered in the light of actual expenses.

The Treasury Notes issued to the same date are as follows :

General currency notes of Five Dollars and over,			180,956,935
do under Five Dollars,	-	-	846,000
Int. bearing at rate 3.65	-	-	1,441,200
do " 7.30	-	-	22,799,900

206,014,035

To pay the balance against the Treasury as above set forth, there must be a further issue of	-	-	26,193,634
And to pay the outstanding requisitions, as above stated			18,524,128

250,761,797

The issue already made of these notes amounts as above shown to	-	-	-	-	-	-	183,244,135
Leaving authority to issue only,	-	-	-				16,755,865

200,000,000

The differences between the balances now due by the Treasury,	-	-	-	-	-	-	44,717,762
and the above	-	-	-	-	-	-	16,755,865

is	-	-	-	-	-	-	27,961,897

Unless this balance can be paid by bonds or 7.30 notes, the authority to issue general currency notes must at once be extended to pay the same; and that authority must be extended still further to meet the appropriations already made by Congress, and not yet paid, and also the further appropriations yet to be made.

The appropriations already made by Congress and not drawn on 1st August, amount to - $ 164,687,389 93

The estimates submitted by the various Departments of the additional supplies required to make good deficiencies and to support the Government to 1st January next, are as follows :

For the War Department,	-	-	-	44,373,590 36
" " Civil list,	-	-	-	386,607 39
" " Miscellaneous,	-	-	-	102,899 38

$ 44,863,097 13

So that the whole amount of supplies required to 1st
January presents a total of - - $ 209,550,437 06

Congress must now determine the best mode of raising this sum.

If the bonds or stock of the Government to any considerable extent could be sold, they would unquestionably offer the best mode of raising the money. An examination of our funded debt account will show that only a small portion can be raised in this way.

The whole amount of bonds and stock issued is as follows:

8 per cent. stock and bonds,	-	-	-	41,577,250
6 " " call certificates,	-	-	-	32,784,400
				74,361,650

This statement, while in the large amount of call deposits, it exhibits its confidence in the credit of the Government, yet, in the small comparative amount of bonds and stock, it shows an indisposition to make investments in that form. We are, therefore, constrained to resort to Treasury Notes as the only mode by which the requisite funds can be raised. This resource has its limits. But it is hoped that with a reasonable economy in making the appropriations, the plans already set in operation will extend those limits, so as to reach to the end of the war.

The inherent objections which attend a Government currency are that it disturbs the standard of value and enhances prices. The facility with which it is created is a constant temptation to excess; and the danger of this excess, together with the doubt of an ability to pay, are the chief causes which affect its credit as a currency.

Thus far, no want of confidence has been exhibited in our currency. It freely circulates everywhere, and the fact that the banking institutions receive and pay out Treasury Notes in their own business is the most certain indication that their credit is unimpaired.

The other cause becomes active only when the total amount of circulation exceeds the usual business wants of the community. It operates without relation to the actual value of the circulation, so that even coin, if it could be kept in a country, would (if in excess) produce the same result. The effect is a necessary consequence of the relation between the whole circulating medium and the whole business and property of the community, and can only be modified by influences upon the cause. Every means, therefore, which will reduce the quantity of circulation becomes important, and should be diligently be sought after.

It was with this view that Congress adopted two measures of relief; one, by which any excess in the quantity of currency might at once be permanently withdrawn and funded in 8 per cent. bonds—the other by which the same effect could be produced for a time, through interest bearing notes and deposits on call. Both plans are working well. The deposits have in fact been a permanent loan at 6 per cent. The interest notes, although current to a certain degree, are usually withdrawn from general circulation as soon as a sufficient amount of

4

interest has accrued upon them to make them valuable as a temporary investment. It must be observed, however, that if this interest should remain in arrear for a long or indefinite time, these notes encounter a difficultly which seriously impairs their value, namely, that of an unproductive investment. Thus, being both unproductive and uncurrent, they will not pass into general use unless the interest bo paid annually. It will be seen that the issue of these notes already amounts to upwards of twenty-two millions. Much of it has doubtless been taken under the belief that the interest would be paid like other interest, and I have encouraged this belief by stating that I would recommend to Congress that the interest should be paid annually. I earnestly hope that Congress will approve this recommendation. The payment could be stamped annually on the note, without encumbering it with a coupon : and in this way it is believed the objects intended by the issue would be effected.

I would also recommend that the notes be issued of a less denomination than one hundred dollars. The large amount of money in the hands of private capitalists is the fund which we must induce to be loaned for the uses of the Government. From the War Tax returns and from estimates as to such States as have not yet made complete returns, this fund may be set down at seven hundred millions, and one of the best means for procuring the use of part of it by the Government seems to be through these notes which answer the double purpose of currency and investment.

I have, also, to report that the acceptance of deposits on call at 6 per cent. has operated well. It will be seen that nearly thirty millions have been deposited in this way; thus proving, at the same time, the confidence of the country in the Government, and the advantages of the plan.

It will also appear from the statements herewith that there have been issued about $846,000 of notes under five dollars. These notes are in great demand, and the issue of them may be extended to ten millions.

The issue of the large amounts and various denominations of notes has confronted us with a difficulty which calls for the intervention of Congress. It requires the services of 129 clerks to perform the various duties involved in the issue of these notes. Of these about 72 are employed in signing; and it will be readily seen that the chief security intended by the signing is thus reduced to but little practical value. It is difficult for any one to bear in mind the signatures of so many different writers; but when to this is added the changes required by sickness, absence, and resignations it becomes impossible.

These embarrassments have been increased by the efforts of our enemies to counterfeit the notes. Organized plans seem to be in operation for introducing counterfeits among us by means of prisoners and traitors; and printed advertisements have been found, stating that the counterfeit notes, in any quantity, will be forwarded, by mail, from Chesnut street, in Philadelphia, to the order of any purchaser.

Under these circumstances, it will be necessary to change many of the plates and to make new issues. The change would be more complete by dispensing with the variety of signatures, which are attached to the other notes. I am informed by the engravers that the signatures of the Register and Treasurer might be engraved in fac simile and printed, and that by stamping an elaborate engraving in colors on the back of the note, the security against counterfeits would be greater than it is at present. The expense of the issue would be diminished by dispensing with the numerous signing clerks, and its more prompt execution would be secured. In order to make this change, the authority of Congress is necessary. The laws against counterfeiting, if not already sufficient, must be made to embrace these notes. In this connection, too, it is proper to bring to the notice of Congress that the penalties of the law, while they apply to any person found in possession of counterfeit blank notes, with intent to utter them, do not seem to embrace notes which are completely filled up and ready for circulation.

The situation of the country made it advisable to remove the printing and engraving establishments from Richmond, shortly after the last adjournment of Congress. The distance from the seat of government at which so delicate a business must now be conducted, involves the necessity of greater expense and of greater ability and higher character than those of ordinary clerks, in those who must superintend. I would, therefore, respectfully suggest that this Department be made a separate bureau, and that a Chief Clerk, with an appropriate salary, be charged with the superintendence of its business at Columbia.

The War Tax has been paid by the several States as follows:

North Carolina,	-	-	-	1,400,000 00
Virginia,	-	-	-	2,125,000 00
Louisiana,	-	-	-	2,500,000 00
Alabama,	-	-	-	2,000,000 00
Georgia,	-	-	-	434,126 12
Florida,	-	-	-	225,374 11
Mississippi,	-	-	-	1,484,467 67
				$10,168,967 90

The State of Georgia has substantially paid in the balance due by her, and the State of South Carolina has paid the whole amount due by her into the Treasury, in the form of six per cent, call certificates. But as the final settlement has not yet taken place, the certificates have not as yet been delivered up, and the account is not yet closed. The returns from the States of Alabama, Louisiana, Mississippi, Arkansas and Texas, have not yet been rendered in complete. The two former States have, nevertheless, paid their taxes in advance.

From the documents furnished, it appears that the States of North Carolina and Alabama, have overpaid their respective assessments, and I will ask leave to submit an estimate of the amounts to be refunded them as soon as the complete returns shall be received.

The collection of the War Tax has presented several difficulties, which it is proper that Congress should have in view, whenever a further tax shall be levied. These difficulties are presented together in a report from the Chief Clerk of the War Tax Office, a copy of which is herewith respectfully submitted. It is also proper to state, that by a judgment of the District Judge of South Carolina, money invested in State bonds has been excepted from the War Tax. An appeal has been ordered from this judgment, but as no Supreme Court has yet been organized, the effect of the judgment will be, to release from any future tax all moneys invested in this form in South Carolina, or in any other State wherein the District Judge may hold the same opinon.

Since the last meeting of Congress, I have appointed three new places of deposit for public moneys, one at Galveston, Texas, one at Knoxville, Tennessee, and one at Augusta, Georgia.

The Assistant Treasurer at New Orleans, has removed his office for the time, to Jackson, Mississippi, and the depositary at Mobile has made a temporary removal to Montgomery, Alabama.

All of which is respectfully submitted,

C. G. MEMMINGER,
Secretary of Treasury.

TREASURY DEPARTMENT,
War Tax Office, August 1st, 1862.

Hon. C. G. Memminger,
   Secretary of the Treasury.

Sir: Believing that the continuance of the war, and the exigencies of the country arising therefrom, will impose upon Congress the duty of providing for another war tax, I feel it my duty to present ·for your consideration some of the views I entertain, which result from my observation of the operations of the act of 19th August, 1861, and to suggest certain amendments which I think should be adopted in the construction of any statute that Congress may enact on this subject.

It is not intended to dictate to you what you should recommend Congress to do in the premises, but merely to lay my suggestions before you, so that, if you perceive any merit in them, you may adopt such as are approved, and present them at the proper time for the consideration and action of Congress.

The returns, so far as received from four States, exhibit an inequality in the valuation of certain species of property, which is unjust in its effects upon a large portion of tax payers, and which, in any future legislation, I think, should not exist. For instance, in the State of Virginia the average value of slaves, according to the ·war tax assessments, is $350 64, while the average in some counties goes up to $400, and in others, falls below $300. The citizens of the latter counties contribute to the general fund for war purposes one fourth less than those of the former. Such inequality is unjust and bears heavily on that class of citizens who are most willing to bear the burden of taxation, and who consequently place upon their property a liberal valuation. Besides, it is calculated to produce murmurings and discontent among the people.

In view of these facts, it seems to me that a uniform rule of valuation for slave property in each State should be incorporated in any future tax law that may be passed, so that those slaves of like age and sex should have a uniform valuation·fixed by the act itself throughout the whole State.

It would be difficult to adjust any uniform scale of classification for real estate, which is affected by so many contingencies and incidents arising from position with reference to marts of trade and commerce, navigable waters, railroads, &c., but with slaves it is different. Those of like age and sex usually maintain the same price within the limits of the same State. In connection with this subject I beg leave to make a quotation from the report of Joseph D. Pope, Esq., Chief Collector of War Tax for the State of South Carolina. He says: "Those persons appointed by the sub-collectors to make the assessment of the property in the State have, doubtless, endeavored to discharge the duties fairly and impartially, and in many instances have given great satisfaction, but in other instances the work has been imperfectly done. This results not so much from the fault of the assessors as from the difference of opinion that will exist as to the value of property by two persons in the same community.

It is respectfully submitted, that by putting a valuation upon slaves by law, according to a classification as hereinbefore referred to, (that is, to fix a scale of value for all slaves in each State according to age, sex and qualifications,) the assessors may be dispensed with entirely, and the expense of that part of the machinery saved. The sub-collector can make his appointments throughout the district and take the returns in the same manner as is now done by the State tax collectors, and he can fix the value of property quite as well as the assessor, and in less time. If a valuation be put upon slaves by law, the only class of property now taxed that would be likely to give rise to a difference of opinion is real estate, and the sub-collector's general knowledge of all lands in his district, with the representations of the owner under oath, aided by the opinion of disinterested persons, would enable him to fix the value for taxable purposes without difficulty. The assessors arrived at their conclusions in the same way in taking the present returns. Large towns and cities may be made an exception, and for them an assessor or assessors may be appointed if necessary."

In addition to these views of Mr. Pope, it may be further suggested that each county should constitute a tax district, except in the case of very large counties, which may be divided into two, and that large towns and cities may be managed in the same way.

The sub-collectors' compensation should be a certain per cent. on all sums under ten thousand dollars say, and a diminished per cent. on all over that amount, and under twenty thousand dollars, and so on, regularly diminishing the per centum as the amount increases, so as to make it his interest to collect the last cent due. It may be objected to the proposition to dispense with assessors, that there would be no tribunal to determine appeals from assessments and applications for a reduction of double tax. This tribunal might be supplied by the appointment of a commissioner for each district from one of the magistrates of the county, binding him by a suitable oath and giving him the usual fees for trying cases. The most serious evil of the present system of assessments is the diversity of opinion among so great a number, and the consequent inequality of valuation of the same species of property, and the inequality of taxation resulting therefrom.

The present law requires each tax payer to deliver a written list of his property. In lieu of this blank printed lists should be supplied to each tax payer by the person receiving the return.

For reasons heretofore expressed in a communication to you, dated 7th April last, I would further suggest that Congress be asked to authorize the appointment of a disbursing agent, to be attached to this office, whose duty it shall be, under the supervision of the secretary, to examine all war tax accounts and settle the same by his requisition on the Treasury, and to make monthly or quarterly statements, as may be deemed most proper, to the first auditor, so that his monthly or quarterly transactions, as the case may be, may be presented in one large account, accompanied by the stated accounts settled by him as vouchers.

All of which is respectfully submitted,
(Signed,)   T. ALLAN,
                                    Chief Clerk of War Tax.

TREASURY DEPARTMENT,

Register's Office, August 4, 1862.

ESTIMATES OF APPROPRIATIONS required for the support of the government for the month of December, 1862, and to meet deficiencies arising prior to 1st December, 1862.

CIVIL LIST.

EXECUTIVE.

For compensation of the President of the Confederate States,	666 66
For compensation of the Vice-President of the Confederate States, - - - - - - - -	316 66
For compensation of the Private Secretary and Messenger of the President, - - - - - -	14 75
For compensation of Secretary of the Treasury, Assistant Secretary, Comptroller, Auditors, Treasurer and Register, and Clerks, Messengers, &c., in the Treasury Department,	53,500 00
For incidental and contingent expenses of the Treasury Department, - - - - - - -	600 00
For compensation of the Secretary of War, Chief of Bureau, and Clerks and Messengers in the War Department -	13,000 00
For incidental and contingent expenses of the War Department, - - - - - - -	5,000 00
For compensation of Secretary of Navy, Clerks and Messengers, - - - - - - -	1,825 90
For incidental and contingent expenses of the Navy Department, - - - - - - -	1,000 00
For compensation of the Postmaster General, Chiefs of Bureaus, and Clerks and Messengers in the Postoffice Department, - - - - - - -	7,442 51
For compensation of the Attorney General, Assistant Attorney General and Clerks and Messengers, - -	1,002 30
For salary of Superintendent of Public Printing, Clerk and Messenger, - - - - - -	362 23
For incidental and contingent expenses of the Department of Justice, - - - - - -	500 00
For incidental and contingent expenses of the Postoffice Department, - - - - - -	1,000 00
For printing for the several Executive Departments, -	10,416 66

TERRITORIAL.

For salaries of Governors and Commissioners of Indian Affairs, and Secretary, Judges, Attorney and Marshals of Arizona Territory, - - - - - -	•808 71
For contingent expenses of Arizona Territory, - -	43 00
Total civil list, - - - - -	$102,899 38

Brought forward, - - - - -	$102,899 88

MISCELLANEOUS.

For light and fuel for the Public Buildings, - - -	6,000 00
For engraving and printing Treasury Notes, Bonds and Certificates of Stock, and for paper for the same, - -	250,000 00
To supply deficiencies in the revenue of the Postoffice Department, - - - - - - - -	130,607 39
Total miscellaneous, - - - - -	$386,607 39

UNDER THE DIRECTION OF THE WAR DEPARTMENT.

For pay of officers and privates of the Army, Volunteers and Militia, and for Quartermaster's supplies of all kinds, transportation and other necessary expenses, - - -	15,638,049 00
For support of prisoners of war, and for rent of the necessary prisons, guard-houses, &c., - - -	200,000 00
For bounty of $50 to each non-commissioned officer, musician and private in the service for 3 years or the war;	3,000,000 00
For purchase of Subsistence stores and Commissary property - - - - - - - -	22,598,041 36
For the Ordnance service in all its branches, - -	2,200,000 00
For the Engineer service, - - - -	200,000 00
For Medical and Hospital supplies, - - -	400,000 00
For pay of Nurses and Cooks other than enlisted men or volunteers, - - - - - - -	48,000 00
For services of Physicians to be employed in conjunction with the Medical Staff of the army, - - -	30,000 00
For the establishment and support of Military Hospitals, -	59,500 00
Total under War Department, - - -	$44,373,590 36

RECAPITULATION.

Civil List, - - - - -	102,899 38
Miscellaneous, - - - -	386,607 39
Under direction of War Deparment, -	44,373,590 36
Total, - - - -	$44,863,097 13

Included in the foregoing estimates are the following for deficiencies arising prior to December 1st, 1862.	
For compensation of Secretary of Treasury, Assistant Secretary, &c., Clerks, &c., -	29,500 00
For incidental and contingent expenses of Treasury Department, - - -	3,000 00
For engraving and printing Treasury Notes, Bonds, &c., and for paper, - - -	185,000 00
For Subsistence stores and Commissary property, - - - - -	15,997,560 11
Total, - - - -	$16,215,060 11

C. T. JONES,
Acting Register.

ESTIMATES *of Appropriations required for the Treasury Department for the Month of December*, 1862, *including deficiencies arising prior to December 1st*, 1862.

The pay per month of all persons connected with the Treasury Department on the 30th of June, 1862, amounted to within a fraction of - - -	24,000 00
The amount required for the payment of salaries for the six months ending December 31st, 1862, provided there be no increase of the force of the Department, will, therefore, be - - - - -	144,000 00
Deduct salary of Secretary paid to October 1st, 1862,	1,500 00
Amount required for the six months, - -	142,500 00
Balances of appropriations July 1st, 1862, available for payment of salaries, - - - -	89,000 00
Required to be appropriated, - - -	$53,500 00
The contingent expenses of the Department average per month, - - - - - -	3,000 00
There will, therefore, be required for the six months,	18,000 00
Balances of appropriations July 1st, 1862, available for payment of contingent expenses, - - -	12,000 00
Required to be appropriated, - - -	6,000 00

Engraving and Printing Treasury Notes, Bonds, &c.

The only data which the Register's office possesses upon which to base an estimate of the amount required for " engraving and printing Treasury Notes, Bonds, &c.," are the accounts of persons engaged in furnishing the Department with Notes and Bonds, from which it appears that the monthly expenditures for this purpose average, - - - -	65,000 00
There will, therefore, be required for the six months on this basis, - - - - - -	390,000 00
Balance of appropriations July 1st, 1862, available for this object, - - - - -	175,000 00
	$215,000 00

Add, to meet any possible increase in the rate of expenditure, -   -   -   -   -   -   35,000 00

Required to be appropriated, -   -   - $250,000 00

C. G. MEMMINGER,
Secretary of the Treasury.

CONFEDERATE STATES OF AMERICA,
WAR DEPARTMENT,
Richmond, July 19, 1862.

Hon. C. G. MEMMINGER,
Secretary of Treasury :

SIR: I have the honor to enclose estimates for the month of December from the Chiefs of Bureau of this Department.
Very respectfully,
Your obedient servant,
GEO. W. RANDOLPH,
Secretary of War.

CONFEDERATE STATES OF AMERICA

WAR DEPARTMENT,

Richmond, July 19, 1862.

Hon. GEORGE W. RANDOLPH,

Secretary of War,

Richmond, Va.:

SIR : Under estimates submitted by myself to your predecessor in office, Congress at its last sitting made appropriations for the civil expenditures of this Department to the 30th of November, 1862, inclusive, and I am now directed to submit further estimates for similar expenditures of the Department up to the 31st of December, 1862.

Under the heads of the respective appropriations I have, therefore, to submit the following as the approximate amounts needed for the period indicated, viz :

For compensation of the Secretary of War, Assistant Secretary of War, Chief of Bureau, Clerks, Messengers, etc.—Thirteen thousand dollars ($ 13,000.)

For incidental and contingent expenses—Five thousand dollars ($ 5,000.)

The appropriations made by Congress at its last sitting for the salaries of the Commissioner and Chief Clerk as well as for the incidental and contingent expenses of the Indian Bureau to the 30th of November, 1862, are believed to be sufficient to meet the further expenses of this Bureau during the month of December, 1862, and that, therefore, no additional appropriation for this purpose is necessary.

I am, very respectfully,

Your obedient servant,

JAMES E. PEEBLES,

Disbursing Clerk, War Department.

QUARTERMASTER GENERAL'S OFFICE,

Richmond, *August* 18, 1862.

Sir : I have the honor to submit herewith an estimate of the amount that will be required for the Pay, Transportation and other allowances provided through this Department for the army for one month, from the 1st to the 31st day of December, 1862, viz. :

Field and Staff for one month,	$ 220,225 00	
25 Regiments Cavalry,	1,265,177 00	
100 Companies Artillery (2 1-2 corps),	435,152 00	
350 Regiments Infantry,	9,221,567 00	
		$ 11,142,121 00

To which add :

For the Transportation of troops and their baggage, of Quartermasters, Subsistence, Ordnance, and Ordnance Stores from the place of purchase to troops in the field ; the purchase of horses, mules, wagons and harness ; the purchase of lumber, nails, iron and steel for erecting store house, quarters for troops and other repairs ; hire of teamsters, laborers, &c., 40 per cent. on the above,   4,368,758 00

To pay for horses of non-commissioned officers and privates killed in battle, under act No. 48, Sec. 7, and for which provision is to be made, -   25,000 00

To pay for property pressed into the service of the Confederate States, under appraisement, and said property having been either lost or applied to the public service, - - - - -   37,500 00

For the subsistence of prisoners of war, under act No. 181, Sec. 1, and the hire of the necessary prisons, guard-houses, &c., for the safe keeping of the same, or so much thereof as may be necessary,   200,000 00

For the bounty of $ 50 to each non-commissioned officer, musician and private now in service for 3 years or for the war, to be paid at the expiration of the 1st year's service on the basis that 60,000 will have to be paid, - - - -   3,000,000 00

For the pay of the officers on duty in the offices of the Adjutant and Inspector General's Department, the Quartermaster General's, Medical, Engineer, Ordnance and Subsistence Departments, -   64,670 00

Total required for one month, - - $ 18,838,049 00

I am, sir, very respectfully,

Your obedient servant, A. C. MYERS,

Quartermaster General.

CONFEDERATE STATES OF AMERICA,

SUBSISTENCE DEPARTMENT,

Richmond, July 17th, 1862.

Hon. G. W. RANDOLPH,
        Secretary of War :

SIR : I have the honor to enclose an estimate for the month of December as required. You will likewise find an estimate for covering the deficiency in the present appropriation, caused by the enhancement of every commodity used of from 100 to 5 or 600 per cent. This has arisen from the fact that this Bureau, as you well know, has never been able to command funds to make provision in advance; not even in amounts adequate to current demands. This matter has been so often brought to the attention of the War Department that it is deemed useless to elaborate upon it.

There likewise appears an estimate of ten millions for the curing of bacon, which should be prepared for now, and in full execution before December. The necessity for that operation last winter when the remnants of salt, from prior importations, were numerous in the warehouses of business men, and the storehouses of individuals and when we possessed all of Tennessee—drew some from Kentucky—and had the productive regions of Virginia and North Carolina, has been fully verified.

Notwithstanding the losses, our armies, both east and west, have been kept in the field by that operation. Now the necessity of a similar proceeding is imperatively indicated.

I am, very respectfully,
        Your obedient servant,
                L. B. NORTHROP.
                Commissary General Subsistence.

AN ESTIMATE *of Funds for the Subsistence of the Confederate States Army for the Month of December,* 1862, *for* 475,000 *men for* 31 *days, making* 14,725,000 *Rations in all.*

14,725,000 rations at 40-75c per ration,	- - -	6,000,437 50
Add ten per cent. for loss, &c.,	- - -	600,043 75
Total amount required,	- - -	$6,600,481 25

Cost of the Ration by Estimate Cost of 100 *Rations.*

Rations.	Articles.	Quantity in Bulk.	Price of.	Amount.
75	Bacon......	37 1-2 pounds...	35c. a p'nd.	13 12 1-2
25	Beef.......	31 1-4 pounds...	20c. a p'nd.	6 25
100	Flour......	150 pounds......	$10 a bbl..	7 65
50	Rice........	5 pounds........	6c. a pound.	30
50	Beans......	4 quarts........	4c. a quart.	16
50	Coffee......	3 pounds........	60c. a p'nd.	1 80
100	Sugar.......	12½ pounds.....	40c. a p'nd.	4 80
100	Candles.....	1 1-2 pounds....	25c. a p'nd.	37 1-2
100	Soap.......	4 pounds........	30c. a p'nd.	1 20
100	Salt.........	2 quarts........	5c. a quart.	10
100	Vinegar....	4 quarts........	30c. a gall'n	30
100	Molasses.....	12 1-2 quarts....	37 1-2 a q'rt	4 68 3-4
				40 74 3-4

L. B. NORTHROP,
Commissary General Subsistence.

AN ADDITIONAL ESTIMATE of *Funds for the Subsistence of the Confederate States Army for the Months of August, September, October and November,* 1862.

The amount required monthly (owing to the greatly enhanced prices of all articles of the ration) is, according to the detailed estimate for December, herewith submitted, -	$6,600,481 25	
Four months here required would then be -		26,401,926 00
Remaining of last appropriation, - -		20,404,365 89
Amount required for time named, - -		5,997,560 11
For the purchase of salt and packing bacon, -		10,000,000 00
Total amount required, - -		$15,997,560 11.

L. B. NORTHROP,
Commissary General Subsistence.

5

SURGEON GENERAL'S OFFICE,

Richmond, Va., July 15th, 1862.

Estimate No. 10.

For medical and hospital supplies from December 1st to
December 31st, 1862, - - - - - - $400,000 00
For the establishment and support of military hospitals
from December 1st to December 31st, 1862, - - 37,500 00

$437,500 00

S. P. MOORE,
Surgeon General.

Estimate No. 11.

For pay of private physicians employed by contract
from December 1 to December 31, 1862,   -   - $30,000 00

For pay of nurses and cooks not enlisted or volunteer
from December 1 to December 31, 1862,   -   -   48,000 00

For pay of Hospital laundresses from December 1 to
December 31, 1862,   -   -   -   -   -   -   10,000 00

For pay of Hospital stewards from December 1 to December 31, 1862, -   -   -   -   -   -   -   12,000 00

                                                $100,000 00

S. P. MOORE,
Surgeon General.

ORDNANCE OFFICE,

July 10*th*, 1862.

ESTIMATE *of Funds required by the Ordnance Bureau.*

Amount required for expenditures for Ordnance service in all its branches for the month of December,
1862,   -   -   -   -   -   -   -   - $2,200,000 00

Amount expended per month during the last twelve
months,   -   -   -   -   - $2,200,000 00

Respectfully submitted,
THOS. S. RHETT,
Col. in charge of Ordnance Bureau.

CONFEDERATE STATES OF AMERICA,

WAR DEPARTMENT,

Engineer Bureau,
Richmond, Va., 15th July, 1862.

Estimate of funds required by the Engineer Bureau for the month of December, 1862,—$200,000, (two hundred thousand dollars.)

A. S. RIVES,
Acting Chief, Engineer Bureau.

CONFEDERATE STATES OF AMERICA,

DEPARTMENT OF STATE,

Richmond, July 10, 1862.

HON. C. G. MEMMINGER,

Secretary of the Treasury :

SIR: I have the honor to acknowledge the receipt of your letter of the 7th instant, relative to estimates of appropriations required for this Department.

The President having determined that the estimates to be submitted to Congress at its extra session in August next, shall be for the month of December, 1862. I have the honor to inform you that the appropriations already voted, are deemed sufficient for the service of this Department to the 1st of January, 1863.

I am, your obedient servant,

J. P. BENJAMIN,

Secretary of State.

CONFEDERATE STATES OF AMERICA,

DEPARTMENT OF JUSTICE,

Richmond, July 11, 1862.

HON. C. G. MEMMINGER,

Secretary of the Treasury :

SIR : I have the honor to submit the following estimates of expenditures for this Department, from the 1st to the 31st December next:

1. For compensation of Attorney General, Assistant Attorney General, Clerks and Messenger, one thousand and two 30–100 dollars.

2. For compensation of Superintendent of Public Printing, Clerk and Messenger in his bureau, three hundred and sixty-two 23–100 dollars.

3. For printing of the several Executive Departments, ten thousand four hundred and sixteen 66–100 dollars.

4. For contingent expenses of Department, five hundred dollars.

5. For salaries of the Governor and Commissioner of Indian Affairs, Secretary, Judges, Attorney and Marshal of Arizona Territory, eight hundred and eight 71–100 dollars.

6. For contingent expenses of Arizona Territory, to be expended by the Governor, forty-three dollars.

Your obedient servant,

WADE KEYES,
Acting Attorney General.

CONFEDERATE STATES OF AMERICA,

POSTOFFICE DEPARTMENT,

Richmond, July 19, 1862.

Hon. C. G. MEMMINGER,

Secretary of the Treasury :

SIR : In compliance with your request of the 7th instant, I have the honor to submit the following estimate of the sums required for the compensation of the Postmaster General, Chiefs of Bureaus, Clerks, Messengers and Laborers, from the 1st to 31st December, 1862:

For compensation of the Postmaster General at,				$6,000 00	$505 43
"	"	"	3 Chiefs of Bureaus, "	3,000 00	758 13
"	"	"	1 Chief Clerk, "	1,500 00	126 35
"	"	"	4 Principal Clerks, "	1,400 00	471 72
"	"	"	1 Disbursing Clerk, "	1,400 00	117 93
"	"	"	24 Clerks, "	1,200 00	2,425 92
"	"	"	31 Clerks, "	1,000 00	2,611 13
"	"	"	1 Topographer, "	1,500 00	126 35
"	"	"	1 Watchman, "	500 00	42 12
"	"	"	2 Messengers, "	500 00	84 24
"	"	"	1 " "	400 00	33 69
"	"	"	3 Laborers, "	1 50 per day	139 50
					$7,442 51

Also an appropriation of $1,000 will be required for the contingent fund of this Department.

I have the honor to be, your obedient servant,

H. ST. GEO. OFFUTT,

Acting Postmaster General.

CONFEDERATE STATES OF AMERICA,

Postoffice Department,

Richmond, July 19, 1862.

Hon. C. G. Memminger,

    Secretary of Treasury :

Sir: In pursuance of an act of Congress, approved April 9th, 1862, I have the honor to submit the following estimate of receipts and expenditures from 1st to 31st December, 1862.

The act of Congress, approved 2nd July, 1836,—now in force—requires that the accounts of the Postoffice Department shall be kept in such manner as to exhibit the amount of its revenues derived from certain sources, and the amount of its expenditures for certain specified objects, but I regret to state that the accounts have not been so kept in the Auditor's office. Therefore, I have not been able to obtain from that office 'the proper official data upon which to base the estimates of receipts and expenditures, (see copy of letter of acting Auditor, herewith annexed,) and have been constrained to base them upon the data in possession of the Department at the time the last estimates were submitted.

Estimated receipts and expenditures from 1st to 31st December, 1862.

For transportation of mails inland, - - -	195,601 31
For compensation of Postmasters, - - -	55,328 26
For Clerks of Postoffices, - - -	9,659 32
For ship, steamboat and way letters. - - -	58 37
For furniture for Postoffices, - - -	1 00
For advertising, - - - - -	350 94
For mail bags, - - - - -	14 25
For paper and blanks, - - - -	1,020 85
For wrapping paper, - - - -	227 36
For mail locks, keys and stamps, - -	38 00
For mail depredations and Special Agents. - -	1,571 45
For miscellaneous payments, - - -	1,963 78
For postage stamps, - - - -	2,824 40
Amounting to, - - -	$268,659 29

RECEIPTS.

From letter postage, - -	$116,987 56	
From postage on newspapers and pamphlets, - - -	20,148 67	
From surplus commissions, - -	915 67	138,051 90
Estimated deficiency from 1st to 31st December, 1862,		$130,607 39

To meet the liabilities of the Department from 1st to 31st December, 1862, an appropriation of $138,051 90, will be required out of any moneys in the Treasury arising out of the revenues of the Department, and to supply the estimated deficiency in the revenues of the Department as above shown, and to enable the Department to meet its estimated liabilities from 1st to 31st December, 1862, it will be necessary for Congress to appropriate out of the General Treasury, the further sum of $130,607 39.

I have the honor to be,

Your obedient servant,

H. St. GEO. OFFUTT,

Acting Postmaster General.

CONFEDERATE STATES OF AMERICA,
TREASURY DEPARTMENT,
First Auditor's Office,
July 18th, 1862.

HON. JOHN L. HARRELL,
Chief of Finance Bureau, P. O D. :

SIR : I regret to inform you that, in consequence of the indisposition of several of the Clerks, and absence from other causes, taken in connection with the removal of the records, temporarily, from the city, and the consequent unavoidable delay in settling and adjusting the postal business of the office—it will be almost impossible to render a concise and accurate statement, to the Postmaster General, in time to enable you to communicate to the Secretary of the Treasury, in accordance with par. 1, chap. 20, act of Congress, approved April 9th, 1862, the estimates for the Postoffice Department of the C. S.

I sincerely trust that the management of the public business, hereafter, may be uninterrupted by similar recurrence, and shall use every effort to render the requisite statement at as early a day as possible.

I am, sir, with great respect,
Your obedient servant,
(Signed.)   J. W. ROBERTSON,
Acting Auditor.

NAVY DEPARTMENT,

July 11th, 1862.

ESTIMATES *of the amount required for compensation of Secretary of the Navy, Clerks and Messenger in his office for the month of December, 1862.*

For salary of the Secretary of the Navy per act approved February 21st, 1861, - - - - - -	$500	00
For salary of Chief Clerk, also Corresponding Clerk and Disbursing Agent, per act approved March 8th, 1861,	175	00
For salary of four clerks, on duty at Navy Department, attached to [the office of Orders and Detail, Ordnance and Hydrography, Provisions and Clothing, and Medicines and Surgery, per section 9 of act approved March 15th, 1861, at $1,500 per annum each, - - -	500	00
For salary of one clerk at $1,500 per annum, per act approved January 14th, 1862, - - - - -	125	00
For salary of two clerks at $1,200 per annum, per act approved March 8th, 1862, - - - - - -	200	00
For salary of one clerk at $1,200 per annum, per act approved January 14th, 1862, - - - - -	100	00
For salary of one clerk at $1,000 per annum, per act approved March 8th, 1861, - - - - - -	84	24
For salary of one draftsman at $1,200 per annum, per act approved January 18th, 1862, - - - -	100	00
For salary of Messenger at $500 per annum, per act approved March 8th, 1862, - - - - - -	41	66
One thousand eight hundred and twenty-five dollars and ninety cents, - - - - - - - -	$1,825	90

S. R. MALLORY,
Secretary of the Navy.

NAVY DEPARTMENT,

July 11*th*, 1862.

ESTIMATE *of the amount required for Incidental and Contingent Expenses of the Navy Department for the month of December*, 1862.

For incidental and contingent expenses of the Navy Department, - - - - - - - - **$1,000 00**

One thousand dollars, - - - - - - - **$1,000 00**

S. R. MALLORY,
Secretary of the Navy.